THE
DIVINE PURPOSE

JOHN MATTHEWS

SOLID GROUND CHRISTIAN BOOKS
BIRMINGHAM, ALABAMA USA

OTHER SOLID GROUND TITLES

We recently celebrated our eighth anniversary of uncovering buried treasure to the glory of God. During these eight years we have produced over 250 volumes. A sample is listed below:

Biblical & Theological Studies: *Addresses on the 100th Anniversary of Princeton Theological Seminary in 1912* by Allis, Machen, Wilson, Vos, Warfield and more.
Power of the Pulpit by Gardiner Spring
Princeton Sermons by Aiken, Green, Hodge, Patton, Warfield
Thoughts on Preaching by James W. Alexander
Notes on Galatians by J. Gresham Machen
The Origin of Paul's Religion by J. Gresham Machen
A Scientific Investigation of the Old Testament by R.D. Wilson
Theology on Fire: *Sermons from Joseph A. Alexander*
Evangelical Truth: *Sermons for the Family* by Archibald Alexander
A Shepherd's Heart: *Pastoral Sermons of James W. Alexander*
Grace & Glory: *Sermons from Princeton Chapel* by Geerhardus Vos
The Lord of Glory by Benjamin B. Warfield
The Person & Work of the Holy Spirit by Benjamin B. Warfield
The Power of God unto Salvation by Benjamin B. Warfield
Calvin Memorial Addresses by Warfield, Johnson, Orr, Webb...
The Five Points of Calvinism by Robert Lewis Dabney
Annals of the American Presbyterian Pulpit by W.B. Sprague
The Word & Prayer: *Classic Devotions from the Pen of John Calvin*
The Christian Warfare by John Downame
A Body of Divinity: *Sum and Substance of Christian Doctrine* by Ussher
The Complete Works of Thomas Manton (in 22 volumes)
A Puritan New Testament Commentary by John Trapp
Exposition of the Epistle to the Hebrews by William Gouge
Exposition of the Epistle of Jude by William Jenkyn
Lectures on the Book of Esther by Thomas M'Crie
Lectures on the Book of Acts by John Dick

To order any of our titles please contact us in one of three ways:

Call us at **205-443-0311**
Email us at **sgcb@charter.net**
Visit our website at **www.solid-ground-books.com**

THE

DIVINE PURPOSE:

DISPLAYED

IN THE

WORKS OF PROVIDENCE AND GRACE;

IN A SERIES OF

LETTERS TO AN INQUIRING FRIEND.

BY

Rev. JOHN MATTHEWS, D.D.
Prof. Theology in Theol. Sem'y, Indiana.

PHILADELPHIA:
PRESBYTERIAN BOARD OF PUBLICATION.

Solid Ground Christian Books
PO Box 660132
Vestavia Hills AL 35266
205-443-0311
sgcb@charter.net
solid-ground-books.com

THE DIVINE PURPOSE
Displayed in Providence and Grace
by John Matthews (1772-1848)

Taken from the 1843 edition published by
The Presbyterian Board of Publication

SPECIAL THANKS: to Wayne Sparkman for his help gathering information on Matthews

First Solid Ground edition December 2009

Cover image is from Ric Ergenbright.
Cover design by Borgo Design, Tuscaloosa, AL

ISBN: 978-159925-239-1

A Memorial Minute
Published in Honor Dr. John Matthews

The peculiar circumstances of Dr. Matthews' early history, give a deep interest to the distinction to which he afterwards attained as a preacher of the everlasting Gospel, and an expounder and teacher of the doctrines of the Church. He was born in Guilford County, North Carolina, in the fall of 1772, where he devoted himself, until advanced to manhood, to a secular occupation, the evidences of which are yet to be seen. The pulpit of the old church in Orange County, where his mind was first turned to the subject of religion, is still pointed out as the handy work of Dr. Matthews.

His academic and theological studies were prosecuted under the direction of the well known Dr. David Caldwell of Guilford, North Carolina, and his license given him by the Presbytery of Orange in the month of March, 1801, at the age of twenty-nine years. Until 1803 he travelled in Tennessee as a missionary, enduring many privations, after which he was called to become the pastor of the Nutbush and Grassy Creek churches of Granville County, North Carolina. In this relation he continued until 1806, when he removed to Martinsburg, Virginia, and then to Shepherdstown, following the removal of Dr. Moses Drury Hoge to Hampden Sydney College.

In this field of labor Dr. Matthews earned a most enviable reputation from the abundance and quality of his ministerial services. His preaching at the commencement of his career as a minister was of a fervent, awakening description. This he afterwards exchanged for a more composed and didactic mode, characterized by great perspicuity and logical arrangement. There is reason to believe that his labors about this time were much blessed to the conviction and conversion of sinners.

From this field of labor and usefulness, where he is yet held in grateful remembrance, he was called to fill the chair of Didactic Theology in the Theological Seminary, then located at

South Hanover, Indiana, now at New Albany. In responding favorably to this call there is evidence to believe that he was actuated by a disinterestedness which shrunk not from the prospect of future trials—"I am called by God," he said to a near friend who was counseling him against the acceptance of the invitation, "to an unpleasant mission like Jonah, and if I do not go I shall expect Jonah's punishment." He left an affectionate people, whose affection he full reciprocated, for a position in which he was called to endure privations until the close of his days. In the spirit of a true disciple he went forth, counting nothing dear to him so that he might finish the work that was given him to do. Happy for the Church if all her ministers were of like spirit.

The same perspicuity which marked his preaching, the intellectual vigor which characterized his work on *The Divine Purpose,* which has so often been studied with profit by the inquiring soul, were manifested in his duties as Professor, and though advanced to the age of seventy-seven, he continued with great vigor of mind, though in great feebleness of body, to attend on all the exercises of the lecture-room. He continued to discharge all his duties as Professor until one week before his decease; then he who had so long and so implicitly listened to his Master's voice while in his earthly abode, was summoned to his mansion of rest on high. He rests from his labors, and his works do follow him.

[excerpted, with minor editing, from *The Minutes of the General Assembly of the Presbyterian Church in the United States of America,* 1848, pages 41-43. Four additional accounts about Dr. Matthews may be found in vol. 2 of Wm. B. Sprague's *The Annals of the American Presbyterian Pulpit* (Birmingham: Solid Ground Christian Books, 2005), pp. 292-299.]

CONTENTS.

LETTER I.

Difference between truth and error always important, ... 9

LETTER II.

The influence of prejudice—answer to the question what are the Decrees of God? 18

LETTER III.

God never acts without design—Providence, what—extends to the preservation of life—and to all inanimate matter, ... 22

LETTER IV.

Death, with all its causes, under the government of providence—the care of God extends to the whole universe, ... 31

LETTER V.

The divine purpose neither suspends, nor violates the free agency of man, ... 40

CONTENTS.

LETTER VI.

The divine purpose perfectly consistent with the free agency of man, ... 50

LETTER VII.

A method of ascertaining the extent of Divine Providence—Great events necessarily include all the less ones, of which they are made up, . . 57

LETTER VIII.

Events, similar to those contained in the prophecies and promises of God, are all included in his purpose, ... 66

LETTER IX.

The purposes of God not inconsistent with the moral agency of man, ... 74

LETTER X.

This consistency incomprehensible to us—but so are many other things which yet we believe, . . 83

LETTER XI.

Moral Government—Salvation by Grace, . . 92

CONTENTS.

LETTER XII.

The favours of God, bestowed according to his own design.—Purpose, decree, intention, foreordination, &c. 100

LETTER XIII.

The number to be saved depends entirely on the will of God, ... 111

LETTER XIV.

The means of salvation suited to each individual, embraced in the divine purpose, . . . 120

LETTER XV.

The providence of God subservient to the designs of mercy—Great events made up of smaller—Our duty and interest to meditate on all his works, 129

LETTER XVI.

Man is a Predestinarian—the Commander of an army—the Architect—the Farmer—elect, foreordain, &c. 143

LETTER XVII.

The final perseverance of Christians, . . . 153

LETTER XVIII.

Same subject continued, ... Page 162

LETTER XIX.

This doctrine gives such views of the character of God as are calculated to excite devotion.—Conclusion, ... 174

PREFACE.

ALTHOUGH the subject, introduced to the attention of the reader in these Letters, is abstruse and difficult, it is here treated in a very intelligible and familiar manner. The chief excellency of these Letters is, that they present the subject of "divine decrees," without that forbidding aspect, which it is apt to assume in the view of many persons. One thing the reader may be assured of, that whether he should coincide in opinion with the author or not, he will find nothing in the volume calculated to wound the most delicate feelings. A spirit of meekness and kindness, eminently characteristic of the writer, pervades the whole.

The doctrine explained and defended, is undoubtedly scriptural; and we should all, without prejudice, cordially embrace it; and where we meet with points which we cannot comprehend, we should bow with humble submission to the dictates of heaven; sensible that our understandings are feeble, and our knowledge small.

At the close of the volume, there are two Letters, replete with solid argument and ingenious illustration, on "the perseverance of the saints." It will be here seen, that the representations commonly given of this comfortable doctrine, by its enemies, are exceedingly distorted, and altogether unjust. When rightly understood it is the very thing which the Christian needs, not only to comfort his heart, but to encourage his efforts. It ought surely to be a pleasing thought that no member of Christ's mystical body shall be broken off; no sheep of his flock be finally lost; for " we are kept by the power of God through faith unto salvation."

A. ALEXANDER.

Princeton,
    New Jersey.

LETTERS

ON THE

DIVINE PURPOSE.

LETTER I.

DIFFERENCE BETWEEN TRUTH AND ERROR ALWAYS IMPORTANT.

Dear Sir—Your letter has been received, in which you request my opinion on various religious topics, for the purpose of aiding you in forming a correct decision, respecting that denomination of Christians with which it would be most expedient to connect yourself. I will endeavour to appreciate, but not abuse, the opinion you are pleased to express respecting my candour and my ability for the performance of such a task. I feel encouraged in this undertaking by the serious intention you express of connecting yourself with that denomination, which, after due deliberation and prayer, shall appear to you most conformable to the sacred Scripture, in its doctrines and form of government. When a person is already determined, it is absurd to ask, and vain to give advice.

It is my duty, and my pleasure, to explain *publicly, and from house to house,* that system of doctrines held by the Church to which I belong. If it pleases God to render these instructions effectual in awakening the careless, in directing the serious inquirer; or in comforting the believer, to his name be the praise. But I sincerely pray, that God, in his mercy, may preserve me from that party spirit, which would lead me to view it as a primary object to make proselytes.

The preceding remark does not imply that there is no difference between truth and error; or that error is not always pernicious, and truth always useful; or that one system of doctrines is not better calculated to excite devout affections in the heart; or that one form of church government does not furnish happier inducements to a religious life, than another. Because we should guard against the influence of party spirit, that is no reason why we should remain the victims of error and delusion; or why we should not, with patience and diligence, inquire after truth. Ignorance and error are the most prolific sources of intolerant bigotry. The history of the church will prove, if I mistake not, that in proportion to the general diffusion of religious knowledge, less of this spirit is perceived, and when the *knowledge of the Lord shall cover the earth, as the waters do the sea*, this spirit shall be driven from the kingdom of Christ: it shall not *hurt, or destroy, in all the holy mountain.* This consideration furnishes additional inducements for inquiring after truth. If we would escape the mortal fangs of this serpent, of this destroyer of Christian peace, let us as much as possible be *filled with all knowledge;* let us *know the truth, and the truth will make us free.* This inquiry should be pursued with an earnest desire for instruction, with humility, with prayer, and with a firm purpose of embracing the truth when discovered: this firmness should be tempered with meekness, forbearance and charity.

I am very far from admitting, that it is a matter of indifference, what system of religious doctrines we receive. It is impossible that opposite doctrines can both be true; and equally impossible that error should answer the purpose, or produce the effects of truth. Error may sometimes mingle, and be received with truth; but still it is error; and still it is pernicious. In proportion to its degree, it will retard the progress of the Christian, and mar the beauty of the divine image on his heart. Truth may be blended with error; but still it is truth; and still it is useful. The disproportion may be so great; error may so far exceed truth, and may relate to such fundamental points, as to prevent altogether the existence of vital piety. The Holy Spirit is a spirit of truth: He never has made, and never will make error and falsehood instrumental in regenerating and purifying the heart. Truth alone is honoured with this instrumentality.

The human countenance is composed of a certain number of features. If these features are regular, and in just proportion, animated with intelligence, beaming with generosity, mildness and love, we call it an interesting and beautiful countenance; we are charmed with its attraction, and prepossessed, at first sight, in its favour. In another, we recognize all the features; but without that regularity and due proportion which would permit us to call it beautiful; and without that sweetness which awakens our complacency. In another, we discover so little of these properties, that we pronounce it the reverse of beautiful and amiable. In some instances a part of the features may be handsome, and others the reverse; in others, some of the features may be entirely wanting, still we call it a human countenance. It is possible to conceive of such an assemblage of parts, though called by the same name by which the human features are, yet so disproportionate, and distorted, as to be frightful; we deny it the character of human; if attached to a human body, we call it a *monster;* if to a different body, we call it a *brute.*

In the moral character of man, a similar variety prevails; some are beautiful with, at least, a distant resemblance of their Saviour; others are deformed with sin. The features of the divine image are drawn on the heart *through sanctification of the Spirit, and belief of the truth.* The word of God is truth. The doctrines of the Bible possess an intrinsic fitness to impress the mind. Each of them, so far as it is understood and believed, will, through the spirit of grace, produce its appropriate effect, awaken its correspondent affection in the soul. These doctrines, taken collectively, constitute that *form,* or *mould,* (Rom. vi. 17.) into which the heart is delivered, by the Great Artificer, that it may receive, and retain all the features and lineaments of his own image. That this " form of *sound,* or *health-giving* (2 Tim. i. 13.) words" may have this effect, we must hold it fast, must cling to it, by faith and love, which is in Christ Jesus. In proportion to the accuracy and extent of our knowledge, and the sincerity of our faith in these doctrines, will be the beauty and perfection of the divine image; we shall possess all those affections and dispositions which belong to the character of Christ; *of his fulness we shall receive, and grace for grace.* If that system of doctrines, which we profess to hold, is but imperfectly understood, then its effects can be but faintly traced on the mind. If it be only some of these doctrines with which we are acquainted, or can be said to know, while of others we are entirely ignorant, then correspondent deficiencies will remain in the character— The mould is complete, but the metal does not come in contact with it. If the system which we receive be mixed with error, then the character will exhibit, not merely deficiencies, but deformities, answering to, and produced by these errors; for the metal will bear the impression of the mould into which it is cast. Error, when believed, will, as certainly as truth, produce its effect. While Christians of all denominations, in proportion as they receive the *sincere milk of the word*, manifest their likeness to the Saviour, and are growing in a meetness for the inheritance of the saints in light; the man, who has never been born again, who receives not the Lord Jesus Christ by faith, whose heart has never melted with evangelical repentance, is destitute of every feature of the divine image. He is led astray by an *evil heart of unbelief;* and is completely under the government of falsehood. No saving truth mingles with that system of error, which is habitually strengthening its grasp, and deepening its impression on his soul. While a divine Agent is imparting his own likeness to the character of Christians, a very different agent, wielding different instruments, is actively employed in imparting his likeness to the character of the sinner. His affections are all fixed on improper objects, or, in an improper degree, on right objects; his dispositions all tend the wrong way. All the features of his moral character are so completely distorted, and so disproportionate, as to exhibit nothing but a frightful and hideous picture of deformity: He is a *monster* in the moral world.

Such is our nature, that the objects, with which

the heart is habitually conversant, and most intimately acquainted, will, as certainly form its character and habits of feeling, as the company, which we keep, will form our manners. By familiar and habitual intercourse with one grade in society, our manners will acquire all that ease and gracefulness which will fit us for the politest circles. In another grade they will acquire nothing but simplicity; which, although not offensive nor disagreeable, yet does not include that artificial polish, which would secure us from embarrassment, if introduced into the higher classes, where greater refinement characterizes the manners. From a still lower grade in society, our manners will acquire a rudeness and vulgarity, unadorned with that simplicity which would exempt such deportment from censure. While surrounded with those of our own grade, whose manners resemble our own, we feel perfectly at ease; of course, most happy. But if accident or business should place us in the midst of those whose manners are polished and refined, their politeness and gracefulness would be distressing to us: the contrast would force upon us a sense of our own deficiencies; and the moment of escape from such society to that of our own level, would be anticipated with real satisfaction. And yet, if our hearts are not as destitute of sensibility, as our manners are of refinement, we shall feel and acknowledge the propriety of accommodating ourselves to the company present. Hence attempts are often made to assume a style of manners with which we are not familiar. Such attempts are generally fruitless; they discover our embarrassment, and set our awkwardness in a more striking point of view.

The preceding remarks may illustrate the effects

to be expected from the different systems of doctrine, now received in the Christian world. These systems represent our own character, and the character of God, with very considerable shades of difference. This difference will operate in forming, if I may speak so, the manners of the heart; that is, its affections, dispositions, tempers and feelings. Some of these systems diminish very much the distance between us and our Maker. By representing our character as less depraved than it really is; our guilt as less atrocious, and dangerous, than truth requires, they proportion the displeasure of God towards us, by that degree of depravity and guilt, with which we are chargeable; our reconciliation, of course, can be the more easily effected; the price of our pardon, if any such be required, need be the less valuable and precious.

In the ordinances of the gospel, we are emphatically said to *draw near to God.* In one sense we are always, independently of our own intentions, in his presence; he is not far from every one of us; for *in him we live, and move, and have our being.* But in these ordinances, we draw near to him, in a religious sense, and under the most important relation of worshippers, for the express purpose of offering to him the devout affections of our hearts. These affections cannot be produced by any mechanical operation; they must be excited, and will be graduated by the views we entertain of ourselves, and of the object of our worship. Our confessions of sin will never exceed the degree of guilt, with which we suppose ourselves to be chargeable; our gratitude will correspond with our estimation of the blessings we receive; our love will glow with no greater warmth than suits our views of the divine benevolence; our sorrow for sin cannot, in the nature of things, exceed our belief of its baseness and hatefulness; our fear of sin, and our watchfulness to guard against it, will be in proportion to our views of the danger to which it exposes us. In proportion as those doctrines which we believe, diminish the guilt of sin, the Saviour will be the less precious to us; because we shall be the less indebted to him, we shall have the less need of his assistance; he will have the less to do, and to suffer for us; we shall feel the less thankful to him. Heaven, which is a state of complete deliverance from sin, will be the less desirable to us; and hell, which is a state of punishment for sin, will be the less dreaded; our exertions to secure the one, and escape the other, will be the less frequent and vigorous. Now these are the affections indispensably necessary in all who worship God, *in spirit and in truth;* and these are the affections which operate as motives of action; which exercise a commanding influence over our daily deportment. Without them, we may go through all the forms of worship; but it will be a body, without the spirit; the form, without the power of godliness. Without them our conduct may be so regular as to escape the censure of man; but, in the sight of God, it will be considered as deficient, and even condemned as criminal, just so far as it flows from any other principle than supreme and sincere love to his character.

It cannot, therefore, be a matter of indifference, what system of doctrines we believe. These doctrines have a connexion with our everlasting happiness, too intimate and too necessary, to admit the supposition. They are the means, used by the Spirit, in exciting our affections, in forming our moral character, and in regulating our life. It cannot be doubted that some of these systems, now held by the disciples of Christ, are better calculated than others to produce these effects; of course, it is the duty of every man, as opportunity permits, to investigate this subject; to compare these systems with the word of God, and firmly to believe that one, which he finds to be nearest the truth. This is the duty, and this the manner of performing it, enjoined by an inspired apostle, *Prove all things, hold fast that which is good.* Every man is required to be useful in judicious and persevering efforts to promote the cause of vital piety; but the zeal with which he employs the means within his power, will be in proportion to the sincerity and fervour of his religious affections; these again, have an intimate and necessary connexion with the doctrines which he believes. One system of doctrine is better calculated to excite these affections, to prompt to these exertions than another, because nearer the truth. The man, who satisfies himself with the reflection, that the system which he holds is, upon the whole, good, and in some degree useful, when by making the proper inquiry, he might discover that another is evidently better, possessing a still greater tendency to be useful, is certainly inexcusable, and of course, culpable, if he fails to make that inquiry.

I, therefore, cordially approve of your intention of examining for yourself, by the only infallible standard—the word of God, those different, and often conflicting systems, now abroad in the world. If you prosecute this inquiry with meekness and humility, and especially with prayer for the divine blessing, I have no doubt, the Holy Spirit will guide you into the knowledge and belief of all truth, as it is in Jesus Christ. I will cheerfully give you my sentiments on the two important doctrines, mentioned in your request—the divine decrees, and the perseverance of the saints.

LETTER II.

THE INFLUENCE OF PREJUDICE—ANSWER TO THE QUESTION, WHAT ARE THE DECREES OF GOD?

No person can have been so long conversant with the world as you have been, without often observing the effects of *prejudice*. It implies the belief of a statement, or opinion, without examination; of course, without a knowledge of the evidence on which the truth of that opinion is founded. A judgment is formed, for which no good reason can be given. In this way, either truth or error may be, and often is, received. It is peculiarly unfortunate when its influence operates in favour of error; for it renders the mind almost, if not quite inaccessible to truth. It is a hopeless undertaking, to reason with men under its influence. You state a case to them, differently from their opinion, and invite them to a fair and candid inquiry; but they have *prejudged* the case; they have no doubts on the subject. They formed their opinion without deliberation, of course, without difficulty, and why should they doubt? Perfectly satisfied with their present views, troubled with no doubts respecting their correctness, they can see no reason for investigation. In the same manner, without inquiry, and without any doubt, they believe that all opinions, differing from their own, are unfounded and erroneous; they, of course, consider all examination as useless and unnecessary. Your proposal, therefore, to inquire, can only excite their passions; which either pervert, or repel, the force of your reasonings; and, in fact, disqualify their minds for any thing like useful investigation. Their opposition to your statements, is that of feeling, and not of the understanding. They consider it as necessary to reject and oppose error, as to hold and defend the truth. Such men are apt to make a convenience of certain vague and general terms, which they consider rather as the signals of a party, than as the signs of definite ideas. If the term is used by the party to which they belong, without conveying one distinct perception to the mind, it awakens all the feelings of approbation; and they are determined to defend it. But if the term is generally used by those whom they consider their opponents, then it awakens all the feelings of disapprobation and hostility; the mind almost instinctively assumes the attitude of resistance; they are determined to oppose it. Their passions are excited, but their understanding is not enlightened.

These remarks, as you have no doubt observed, have been often verified, during the prevalence among us of party spirit on the subject of politics. But the effects of prejudice appear on no subject more frequently than on that of religion; and especially respecting the divine decrees. There are multitudes in whose minds the very term, *decree*, is sufficient to excite the liveliest feelings of dislike and opposition.

I am to offer you my sentiments on the subject of the divine decrees. May God, in mercy, grant that spirit of meekness, humility, and wisdom, without which the inquiry will be prosecuted to no advantage! I am not undertaking to clear this doctrine of all difficulties; or to render it, in all its bearings and connexions, comprehensible to your mind. What I chiefly intend is to furnish you with that mode of reasoning, and with that train of reflection, which has led my own mind to believe in this doctrine, as taught in the word of God.

About the middle of the seventeenth century, an assembly of Divines, convened at Westminster, in England; composed two catechisms, the one called the larger, and the other, the shorter catechism; both of which are received by the Presbyterian Church, as excellent compends of Christian doctrine. A question in the shorter catechism brings the subject now under consideration, fully and distinctly to view: *What are the decrees of God?* Nor do I know of any thing, within the same compass, more to the point or more satisfactory, than the answer to this question: *The decrees of God are his eternal purpose, according to the counsel of his will, whereby, for his own glory, he hath fore-ordained whatsoever comes to pass.*

In this answer, the *decrees* of God and his *purpose*, are considered the same: the one is explained by the other, and both are again expressed in the term, *fore-ordained.* To decree, to purpose, to fore-ordain, to predestinate, to predetermine, when used to express the intentions, designs, and plans of God, are so nearly if not altogether the same in their meaning, that they will be considered as such, and will be used as synonymous terms. The words, decree, purpose, fore-ordination, &c., will be considered and used also as meaning the same thing. Those events, or actions, to which the divine purpose relates, may be expressed, with equal propriety, either by the term decreed or purposed, or fore-ordained, or predestinated, or designed, or predetermined. These purposes of the Almighty are neither capricious nor arbitrary: they are not capricious; because they are formed, or more properly, they exist in the divine mind, according to a perfect rule, which is his own will. From this they derive both stability and unity. They are not arbitrary; since he does not ordain an event merely because he has power to accomplish it; they are according to the *counsel* of his own will. Of all the works of God, it is said, *in wisdom hast thou made them all.* All things, and all events are embraced in these decrees; for *his kingdom ruleth over all:* and by him *all things do consist,* or hang together. All these determinations have respect to his own glory, as their chief and ultimate end; and will all terminate in that glory—the highest and best end which can be proposed. According to the conceptions of our finite capacities, these purposes must exist in the divine mind before the events to which they relate are brought to pass. If they exist one day, or one hour before, as it respects God himself, to whom one day is as a thousand years, and a thousand years as one day, it is precisely the same as if they existed from all eternity. These purposes are, therefore, eternal. Now, each part of this answer appears to be worthy of all acceptation; because the whole of it is founded on Scripture, and agrees perfectly with all we know of the character of God, and of the government which he exercises over the world. I, therefore, receive it, not only because it is true, but also because it is useful and comfortable.

If, however, you feel any difficulty in receiving, as true, the above statements, you will admit the truth of the two following propositions, viz.:

That the government of the universe is in the hands of Jehovah: or that *his kingdom ruleth over all;* and that, *by grace ye are saved.* If you receive these two propositions, then, in my opinion, you are a genuine Calvinist; for they embrace the very essence of that system. The former of these may be understood as including the works of creation and providence; the latter as referring to the work of redemption. But all who profess to believe the Bible, believe these propositions, for they are parts of that volume; and yet all are not Calvinists. Our only difference, therefore, is respecting the meaning of these, and similar passages of Scripture. The first of these will be considered in my next letter.

LETTER III.

GOD NEVER ACTS WITHOUT DESIGN—PROVIDENCE, WHAT—EXTENDS TO THE PRESERVATION OF LIFE—AND TO ALL INANIMATE MATTER.

In your evening walk you tread on a worm, and crush it to death; presently you observe a venomous serpent near your path, which you also kill. In the first case, the effect, as it respected yourself, was accidental; that is, it happened without your intention; you had no design to injure the worm. But in the latter, the effect, or event, was according to your intention; your killing the serpent was in consequence of a design, previously and deliberately formed, in your mind. And yet, in both cases you were the cause of death. In a thousand instances, the exertions of men produce effects, not only without design, but contrary to their deliberate intentions. But nothing like this can possibly happen with God. It would be the height of absurdity, and manifest the greatest ignorance of his character to suppose, that his power was exerted in blind efforts, and was producing effects, which he had not previously designed. Every effect which his power produces, is according to the predetermination of his own wisdom.

It is probable, if not certain, that the whole system to which this earth belongs was created at the same time. The sun, which is the common centre, and the moon are expressly mentioned. The supposition is very much strengthened by the Mosaic account, in which, besides mentioning the sun and moon, it is distinctly stated *he made the stars also;* that is, at the same time. Not the fixed stars; but those planets, commonly called stars, which are known to revolve round the sun, with this earth. In the beginning, God created the heavens and the earth; not by accident, but from design. In that plan, which guided his creative power, were embraced all the parts of these heavens, and this earth. The number of planets, belonging to the system; their distance from each other; their revolution; their figure and dimensions; were all decreed with absolute certainty. If then this purpose existed in the divine mind previously to creation, there is no alternative, but to believe that it is an eternal purpose. To suppose any thing else, involves an absurdity too great to impute to any man.

No objection, however, will be made, I presume, to the creation of the world, according to an eternal purpose of God, but chiefly to his governing the world, in the same manner; and yet this, if I mistake not, is included in the proposition, which you will readily admit, that the government of the universe is in the hands of Jehovah, or that his kingdom ruleth over all. This government and his providence are the same. Every effect, and every event, to which his providence extends, are so many particulars included in his government. Now, consider for a moment, what a vast variety of events are in Scripture most explicitly ascribed to God; and which, of course, are under the control of his guardian care. But in what sense can an event be ascribed to God, unless it is brought to pass by his agency? It is true, divine providence is carried on by the instrumentality of second causes: but this fact cannot alter the case. These second causes, whether they be rational or irrational creatures, with or without life, are completely dependent on the Almighty, and could neither exist nor act without his powerful and constant support. Their preservation, and the employment of their instrumentality, are important parts in the plan of his providence. Hence the propriety of using the term PROVIDENCE, which means foresight, or care respecting future events, so as to secure their occurrence, at a particular time, and under particular circumstances. Thus when one effect is produced, care is taken that it may answer the purpose of a second cause, or be instrumental in producing a second effect, and this again a third, &c. throughout a series of causes and effects, which may terminate only with the end of the world. In producing the first effect, provision was made for the second, in the second, for the third, &c. That effect, which is here considered the first, was itself produced by another which preceded it, and this also by another; and thus the unbroken chain may be traced up, through all the intermediate links, to the First Cause. In the first effect, produced immediately by the hand of God, provision was made for all that were to flow from it, down to the last. Thus, the first and the last event, of any given series, are connected together; the last is dependent on the first, as the first is on God. A second cause necessarily implies a first, on which the whole connexion, in all its parts, and in every stage of its progress, is dependent. Every intervening effect was, from the beginning, as distinctly in his view, and as certainly embraced in his purpose, as the first. One view, and one purpose, pervades the whole. The Providence of God is, therefore, his unerring and perfect foresight; his wise and guardian care, extending through a vast concatenation of causes and effects, from the first to the last moment of time—a successive flow of events, which none can arrest, but He who first set it in motion.

For the sake of illustration, let some particular case be selected. The preservation of human life is known to depend on the concurrence of a great variety of means, or second causes; man's own exertion and prudence, food, water, air, clothing, medicine, &c., and yet, in Scripture, this preservaton is ascribed in the most explicit and unequivocal language to God. " O thou preserver of men; O Lord thou preservest man and beast; in him we live, and move, and have our being." Job vii. 20; Ps. xxxvi. 6; Acts xvii. 28. Creation is not ascribed to God in language more intelligible and more explicit than this. The life of man, however, is preserved, generally, not by miracle, but by providence; that is, by the use of means, possessing, in themselves, a fitness to answer the intended purpose. The preservation of human life necessarily implies the provision of all those means on which that life depends.

The preservation of the apostle Paul's life, as far as we can judge, at one time depended on his nephew, who, accidentally, as we call it, but providentially, in the purposes of God, heard the bloody intentions of the Jews; of which he gave immediate information to the chief captain. (Acts xxiii. 16, et seq.) Had this captain been a Gallio, still the effect would have taken place. But he was not; provision was made in his character, and in the dispositions of his heart for acting promptly on this information; and thus securing Paul from these murderous designs. Had this young man been at a distance, he could not have heard this conversation; of course, could not have given the information. But He who had determined to prolong the life of the distinguished apostle, determined also to secure the presence of his nephew, at the proper place and at the proper moment. At another time, his life, and the life of the whole company, depended on the continuance of the sailors in the ship. "Except these abide in the ship ye cannot be saved." And yet he had been previously assured that his life should not be lost. The intention to preserve him, included the exertions of the seamen, as the means of that preservation.

The preservation of life often depends on circumstances too trivial to excite the least attention at the moment; yet such occurrences are sometimes the shield by which man is secure from death. While the Rev. Dr. Rodgers, late of New York, lived at St. George's, in Maryland, one of his neighbours determined to murder him. "Accordingly the miserable wretch made every preparation for executing his nefarious purpose. He watched the motions of Mr. R. with a loaded musket, day after day, for a considerable time, and eagerly sought for a favourable opportunity to destroy his life. He waylaid him when he rode abroad. He hovered about his door, at intervals, by day and night. But something always occurred to carry the object of his pursuit in a different direction from that which was expected, and thus to avert the intended mischief."* The Doctor knew nothing of these attempts; and, therefore, could have no design to avoid the danger. But the great Head of the church intended to employ him still longer in his vineyard; and, therefore, at the proper moment, and in due proportion, all the motives and all the circumstances necessary to his preservation, were ready and brought into operation. A very slight change in these occurrences might have carried him on to instant death.

This wise and gracious care of the Almighty Father extends to all the human family, every individual of which, is equally, and at all times dependent on him. Whatever God performs in the course of his providence, we ought to believe that from the beginning it was his intention to do. If that intention preceded the event, as it must have done, then we cannot avoid the conviction that, in the divine mind, it existed from all eternity. In this eternal purpose is included the preservation of every human being; and, of course, all the means necessary for the support of life. If the means should fail, life also must fail, unless it be preserved by miracle, which we are not to expect. If, in the divine purpose, the end is rendered cer-

* Miller's Life of Rodgers.

tain, so also are the means. No human being can long subsist without food. If God has determined to preserve, for a given time, the life of any particular man, he must also have determined to provide that food without which he cannot live. Nor is this food produced by miracle; its production depends on other causes; on the fertility and cultivation of the soil; on the influence of the sun, the rain, &c. If, then, he determined to provide the necessary food, he determined also to secure the operation of all those causes on which the production of that food depends. The causes which are instrumental in furnishing bread, are themselves the effects of other causes which preceded them, and these again of others, till we are led up to the great First Cause. Thus we are taught to pray to our Father in heaven for our *daily bread.* But why pray to him for it, unless its provision depends on his wisdom and his care? The causes on which the provision of this bread depends, are also ascribed to him. "And God said, let the earth bring forth grass, the herb yielding seed, and the fruit tree yielding fruit, after his kind." Gen. i. 11. "He maketh his sun to rise on the evil and on the good, and sendeth rain on the just and on the unjust." Matt. v. 45. If the preservation of our life requires bread, for this bread we are taught to pray, and thus to acknowledge it as one of his blessings. If this bread is produced by other means, these means are instruments in the hand of Omnipotence, employed for this special purpose. All second causes are the servants of the Supreme Ruler, waiting on him in readiness to perform his will.

In the same manner, all living creatures depend on God for their preservation. "O Lord," said the

Psalmist, "thou preservest, not only man, but beast also. These wait all upon thee, that thou mayest give them their meat in due season." Psal. civ. 27, 28. All the beasts of the field, the fowls of the air, the fishes of the sea, together with every living thing, by whatever name it is called—are all sustained by the providential care of the great Creator. "God feedeth the ravens. Thou openest thy hand, they are filled with good; thou hidest thy face, they are troubled. Thou satisfiest the desire of every living thing." Psal. cxlv. 16. Not one of them is forgotten before God. If this language means any thing, it means that this whole department of animated nature, from the greatest to the very least, is sustained in being by divine power, wisdom, and goodness. Food is as necessary for the support of their life, as for the life of man. This food must be suited to their nature; and their natures are very different from each other. Some are carnivorous; some are graminivorous. That which is received by one, is rejected by another. This food must not only be suited to their nature, but must be given in due season. The purpose of God, to preserve the life of all these myriads of living creatures, certainly implies his purpose of securing for them all the various kinds of food, from which the nourishment of life may be derived. It also renders certain the concurrent instrumentality of all those means, or second causes, on which the provision of this food depends. Here again, in attempting to trace the succession of causes and effects, we are carried up, and lost in the counsels of infinite wisdom, which must for ever exceed our limited comprehension.

In Scripture, we are taught to believe that the providence of God extends to the whole vegetable kingdom; and indeed to every part of inanimate nature. The fruitful earth is still, and has been in every age, obedient to the mandate of Jehovah. "He causeth the grass to grow for the cattle, and the herb for the service of man; he hath planted the cedars of Lebanon." He not only causes the grass and all kinds of herbage to grow; but he also clothes that grass, and this herbage. Neither their number, their shape, nor their colour, are either uncertain or contingent, but determined by the wise and eternal purposes of Him who causes them to spring from the earth. He gives the grass its form and its verdure; to his pencil the lily, the rose, the pink, &c. are indebted for all their discriminative tints, and their brilliancy of colour. If he plants the cedars of Lebanon, so, by fair and undeniable consequence, does he plant the trees of every other kind, over the whole earth. The oak, the pine, the willow, &c. are as much dependent on his care as the *lign-aloes* and the cedar.

Inanimate matter, in all its combinations and forms, in all its movements and operations, is completely subject to the controlling hand of Omnipotence. The wind bloweth where it listeth, as to any power in man, to direct its course, or stop its progress, but not without the command of God; for "He bringeth the wind out of his treasuries; it is his wind; he causeth it to blow." When Jonah fled from his duty, the Lord sent out a great wind into the sea after him, and he was soon brought to repentance. When it has answered the purpose for which it is sent out, then "He stayeth his rough wind, and gathereth it in his fist. He scattereth the hoar frost like ashes. Fire and hail, snow and vapour," whether they sweep over the earth with desolating fury, or minister to the comfort and convenience of man, are only fulfilling his word. Even the resistless thunder-bolt, shivering with equal ease the palaces of kings, and the trees of the forest, is launched and guided by his hand; for "He directeth his lightnings to the ends of the earth." See him at one time measuring the waters in the hollow of his hand; at another, meting out the heavens with a span; now, comprehending the dust of the earth in a measure; again, weighing the mountains in scales, and the hills in a balance; and who can suppress the devout exclamation, O Lord! how manifold are thy works; how vast, how boundless the extent of thy providence! Matter, it is true, is governed by what we usually call the laws of nature; but what are these laws, but the power, the wisdom, and the goodness of God, producing with regularity and certainty, all the diversified phenomena, which strike our attention?

LETTER IV.

DEATH, WITH ALL ITS CAUSES, UNDER THE GOVERNMENT OF PROVIDENCE—THE CARE OF GOD EXTENDS TO THE WHOLE UNIVERSE.

If the great Jehovah is continually employed in preserving the life of man, must not the termination of that life be ascribed also to him? Have we the consolation of believing, that divine wisdom presides over all the changes which diversify our life, regulating the minutest events connected with our safety, numbering even the hairs of our head; but, in the hour of death, shall we be cast off, and be altogether deserted by our merciful Father? Reason, and the word of God, unite in forbidding us to admit the gloomy conclusion; and in authorizing us to cherish the belief that the last hour, the last moment of life, is as certainly embraced in the designs of his providence, as any of those hours or moments that are past. The divine purpose to preserve our life is not vague and indefinite as to time. We have abundant reason to believe that the length of our life, as well as its preservation, is determined by the wisdom of Him who cannot err. He alone has the right, and he alone is competent to decide when it is most proper to withdraw from us his supporting hand.

In Scripture, we find this event is ascribed to God. "I know," said the pious and afflicted Job, that "thou wilt bring me to death. The Lord killeth; he bringeth down to the grave." 1 Sam. ii. 6. "Is there not an appointed time for man upon earth? Yes, verily, his days are determined, the number of his months is with thee; thou hast appointed his bounds, that he cannot pass." Job. vii. 1, and xiv. 5.

If this event should for a moment be supposed to depend not on the will of God, but of man; that each individual should possess the power to prolong his life according to his own pleasure; this would also imply the power to command all those means by which life is sustained. If he cannot by his own power secure those means, neither can he preserve his life; for it cannot be preserved without them. He must have it in his power to provide food: for without it, he cannot long subsist. This requires an absolute control over all those causes on which the provision of food depends. He must impart fertility to the earth, must command the sun to shine and the rain to fall; for

THE DIVINE PURPOSE. 33

without these the earth will not yield her increase. These causes are the effects of others which preceded them; and these again of others; and thus the connexion may be traced back hundreds of years, before any man now living was born. This supposition would require him to act hundreds or even thousands of years before he existed. Nothing, therefore, can be more absurd than to suppose man capable of performing all this; and yet if he cannot do all this and much more, neither can he prolong his own life; and if he cannot prolong his own life, neither can he determine, independently of the divine will, his own death. Life and death are in the hands of the same being; and that being must exercise the most absolute control over all those causes which contribute to the support of life. That being can be none other than Jehovah.

If it depended on our own choice, how few of us would ever leave this world? Even under accumulated evils, we generally cling to life with the most eager endearment. To produce in the human mind a desire to depart, is among the sublimest effects of genuine piety. The language of this desire, however, is, " all the days of my appointed time will I wait, till my change come;" for it is always connected with perfect submission to the will of God.

Death itself is not only ascribed to the great Disposer of all events, but also all those causes which generally issue in the termination of life. Thousands of the human family are annually swept off by diseases of various kinds, all of which may be included in the term pestilence. This is so frequently, and under such a variety of circumstances ascribed to God, that it is almost needless to mention particular passages. " I will smite them with the pestilence; he gave their life over to the pestilence; I have sent among you the pestilence." Numbers xiv. 12. Psalm lxxviii. 50. Amos. iv. 10. This pestilence, walking in darkness, and wasting at noonday, is but the servant of the Almighty, and cannot move or affect the life of a single creature without his command. If, however, it should not be admitted that the pestilence includes all diseases, still we find in Scripture that, collectively and singly, they are subject to the regulations of divine power and wisdom. " The Lord will make thy plague wonderful, and sore sickness, and of long continuance; also every sickness, and every plague, which is not written in the book of this law, them will the Lord bring upon thee, until thou be destroyed." Deut. xxviii. 60, 61. The truth here asserted is, that all kinds of diseases are sent by the Ruler of the world, and are subject to the guidance of his providence. Of this truth the Divine Redeemer furnished, while on earth, the most conclusive proof, by healing all manner of diseases, which he could not have done, if they were not obedient to his will.

Disease itself is the effect of other causes, which are also ascribed to God. The cause of disease is often generated in the atmosphere. Noxious qualities exhaled from the earth, combine with the air which we breathe; and when thus impregnated, the wind has only to pass over us and we are gone. Shall we suppose that these exhalations rise by chance, and are not included in the divine purpose? Such, no doubt, is the opinion of some. The spirit of inspiration, however, has taught us otherwise, ascribing their rise to the same wisdom which presides over the rise and fall of empires. This vapour, eventually the cause of death, does but fulfil his word. "He causeth the vapours to ascend from the ends of the earth." Psal. cxxxv. 7. If their ascent is regulated by his will, so are all their subsequent movements and effects.

Thousands of mankind have been destroyed by famine; another of those means sometimes used by the Most High in accomplishing his designs. "Arise and go," said Elisha to the woman, "for the Lord hath called for famine," which accordingly came. That sore and grievous famine which prevailed in Egypt, was established by the purpose of God, and came, because he called for it. Gen. xli. 32. Psal. cv. 16. Famine is also produced by second causes, all of which are embraced in the divine plan. If it be occasioned by drought, it is He who "stayeth the bottles of heaven, and bindeth up the waters in his thick cloud." If it be occasioned by storms, these, while desolating the fields, are only fulfilling his word, who has only to speak, and it is done. If it be the consequence of locusts or other devouring insects, he need only issue his proclamation, and "the locusts come, and caterpillars without number;" let him but hiss for the fly, and it is ready to perform the work of ravage. Whenever it pleases God to visit a nation with famine, all the causes by which it is usually produced, are in obedience to his will. The time, the degree, and the result of their operation, are all detailed in those plans of wisdom by which he governs the world.

War is another engine often employed to bring man to his end. While we are bound to believe, on the authority of Scripture, that pestilence, disease and famine, perform their work in obedience to the divine command, can we, with equal clearness and satisfaction, perceive that the rise, the progress and desolations of war are subject to the same control? If there was to be "war with Amalek from generation to generation," it is because "the Lord hath sworn that he will have it." If many of the Hagarites fell down slain, it was "because the war was of God." Exod. xvii. 16. 1 Chron. v. 22. When David was to be chastised for his criminal imprudence in numbering the people, war was one of the scourges offered to his choice. Had war been his preference, we have the same reasons to believe, that this would have been sent, as that the pestilence was actually sent from the Lord. We have, therefore, the same reasons for believing that the rage of war is as certainly directed and limited by an Almighty arm, that we have for believing that pestilence and famine are thus directed and limited. When his purposes are accomplished, then " he maketh war to cease unto the end of the earth." The death of those who fall by the sword, is embraced in the providence of God equally with those who die by disease.

Nor are we destitute of authority for ascribing to the Arbiter of nations even the causes of war. He must, of course, exercise his power over these causes, as well as over that war which is their effect. "Blessed be the Lord my strength," saith the Psalmist, "who teacheth my hands to war, and my fingers to fight." If it originates in the wrath of man, "surely the wrath of man shall praise thee, the remainder of wrath thou shalt restrain." "The king's heart," that is, his passions, dispositions, designs, &c., "is in the hand of the Lord, as rivers of water: he turneth it whithersoever he will." Psal. cxliv. 1.—xlvi. 10. Prov. xxi. 1.

THE DIVINE PURPOSE. 37

It appears, from this induction of particulars, that we are justified in believing that death, with all the means by which it is produced, is constantly under the direction of an overruling providence, which controls, with unerring certainty, all their movements and effects; not with respect to a few only, but to every individual of the human family. Any other supposition, as it appears to me, must and will involve us in absurdities. If one single circumstance, contributing to the death of any person should not be under the control of heaven, under whose shall we place it? Matter has no intelligence, can exercise no thought, and is, therefore, incapable of forming a design to move, or produce any effect whatever. Noxious vapours have no intention of rising from the earth, mingling their unhealthy qualities with the air, and thus producing disease and death. The earth, the sun, and the clouds, hold no consultation, in order to produce a famine for the destruction of man. To suppose that man, independently of divine aid, has any commanding influence over the causes of his own death, has already been proved impossible. Shall we, then, ascribe such an agency to angels? They are expressly said to be ministering spirits, under the government of God, sent forth for the execution of his plans. They possess no independent agency. They, with all the powers they possess, are as completely dependent on God, as the worm that crawls on the earth. Why, then, should they be supposed capable of dividing the government of the world with their Creator? For if men or angels, by an independent power of their own, determine one single event, over that event they would govern; of course, it could not be under, nor even belong to the government of God. Then his kingdom would *not* rule over all: here would be one event, together with its governor, completely independent of his power. There is no being in existence capable of exercising an independent power but one, that is God.

The death of all other animals is included in the wise and comprehensive designs of the Almighty. They are all his creatures, and share in his fatherly regard. Man, for his own amusement, may destroy the life of a sparrow; the hawk may seize and devour it; the serpent may crush it in his coil; but each of these are but instruments in the hand of God, employed in accomplishing his purposes; " for one sparrow shall not fall on the ground," that is, die, " without your Father." If this be true, respecting the sparrow, by the fairest inference, it is also true of all the fowls of the air; and, indeed, of every living creature: all are equally under the notice of his eye, and surrounded by his providence. If they are troubled, according to the beautiful language of the Psalmist, it is because " thou hidest thy face;" if they die, and return to their dust, it is because " thou takest away their breath."

I hope, before this time, you have seen that in Scripture, a wider range is given to the providence of God, than would readily be admitted by a person not accustomed to reflect on the meaning of those passages which relate to the subject. The whole world, with all its inhabitants, and all its events, is embraced in that range. An all-wise and Almighty being created, sustains, and governs the whole for his own glory. Those who deny, as some do, that God has any thing to do with some events which take place among men, must, of course, deny that the providence of God extends to these events; for his providence necessarily implies the exercise of his power, in some way or other, in bringing these events to pass. Providence is not an attribute of Deity, but the manner in which his attributes, especially his wisdom, power, and goodness, are employed in governing the world.

Although the above remarks relate chiefly to this world, yet there can be no doubt but the great Sovereign exercises the same paternal care over every other part of the universe. If those planets, which make a part of that system to which our earth belongs, be inhabited, as modern philosophy supposes, over all their inhabitants, over all their actions, and over all their changes, which in any manner affect their existence, the eternal Jehovah watches with a sleepless eye, and guides them with an unwearied and invincible hand. To each individual, and to each event, his guardian providence extends, with as much accuracy and ease, as if that individual, and that event were the only objects which engaged his attention. Modern astronomers consider it probable that all those lucid points, called fixed stars, are, in reality, so many suns, like the one which enlightens our globe, and makes our day; that these suns are centres, around which systems of worlds revolve; and that these worlds are all inhabited, by creatures of various orders. If this be admitted as probable, the Bible teaches us to view the Almighty Parent as watching over, sustaining, and governing all these worlds, and all their inhabitants, and all their actions, and all the circumstances which diversify their existence. Not only these worlds and their inhabitants, but a detail of events, from the greatest to the least, is embraced by his plan, in the execution of which his hand is continually employed. "Great and marvellous are thy works, Lord God Almighty; just and true are thy ways, thou King of saints."

LETTER V.

THE DIVINE PURPOSE NEITHER SUSPENDS NOR VIOLATES THE FREE AGENCY OF MAN.

It has not escaped my recollection that there are many objections advanced against the sentiments contained in the preceding remarks; some of which are founded on misapprehension, others relate to what is really incomprehensible to our limited capacities. There are many who believe, without hesitation, that the world was created by the power of God. Here they understand the general term, *world*, in its proper sense, as including each and every particular belonging to the world. In the meaning of this complex term, they include each man, animal, or living creature, each tree and plant, and atom of matter. As it regards creation, they do not object to the minutest detail of particulars. Probably they will not object to the statement that God is the Governor of the world; but they will not understand the term, *world*, in the same sense as in the former case; but in a vague, indefinite sense, of which the mind can form no distinct idea. If you mention particulars, for instance, certain events brought to pass by the agency of men, objections will soon be made. Now, what we ask, and have a right to claim, is, that they will understand the term in the same sense in this case as in the former; as including all the particulars belonging to this complex term, when used in relation to the divine government. If we admit that the world is governed by the Almighty, if we understand the word correctly, we admit that all the particulars, that is, that each individual, and each event belonging to the world, are governed by him; for the world is made up of these particulars.

For the sake of illustration, let us take another term, also complex; that is, including a number of particulars, in its meaning; but of less extent than the term world. " Art thou not God in heaven, and rulest not thou over all the kingdoms of the heathen; and in thine hand is there not power and might so that none is able to withstand thee?" 2 Chron. xx. 6. In the meaning of the term kingdom, is necessarily included a number of men, divided into rulers and subjects, living under a system of laws. Abstract men from the idea of a kingdom, and what will remain? nothing; for without men there can be no kingdom. When therefore it is stated, that God rules over a kingdom, the meaning is that he rules over the men who compose that kingdom. Again; what idea does the term, man, convey? Does it not include his thoughts, his passions, and his actions? If these be separated from man, what will be left as the subject of government? A soul indeed, but without thoughts or passions; a body, indeed, but without actions. If these are not included in the idea of man, there is nothing left which can be governed. Therefore when we say the government of God is exercised over man, we mean, or at least we ought to mean, that it is exercised over his thoughts, his passions, and his actions. If it be not exercised over his thoughts, &c., it cannot be exercised over man; and if not over each individual man, it cannot be over a kingdom; for without men, there can be no kingdom. To govern in any sense, is to secure a conformity, in the subject of government, to some law, or rule. The government of a father, over his family, means his inducing them to conform themselves to his will, which is the rule. If they disobey this law, they are no longer governed by him; for they cannot be governed by a law which they transgress. He, of course, can be said to govern them no further than he can secure in their conduct, a conformity to his will. So the divine government means the exercise of power sufficient to secure, in the subjects of his government, a conformity to his will. But the government of God is exercised over the thoughts, passions, and actions of men. The result is, that the thoughts, &c., of men, are subject to the influence of such decisive control, as to secure a conformity to his providential purposes. Nor is it possible for any creature to disobey this government, which, to distinguish it from that which is moral, I will call the Government of his Providence. Part of the passage of Scripture last quoted will abundantly support this declaration. Such also, if I mistake not, is the meaning of Isaiah; "My counsel shall stand, and I will do all my pleasure: yea, I have spoken it, I will also bring it to pass; I have purposed it, I will also do it." Isa. xlvi. 10. The meaning of these, and many similar passages, is, I confess, to my mind, not very obvious when understood as relating to the moral government, the laws of which are shamefully and repeatedly transgressed; but clear, forcible, and undeniable, when understood as relating to those wise and eternal purposes, according to which the providence of God is uniformly conducted.

Other objections against the doctrine arise from the difficulty of reconciling it with the free agency of man; and you have more than intimated that this was your own case. Many others have felt the same difficulty, who have acted very differently from what you have, or, I trust, ever will do: for this reason, they have rejected the doctrine altogether. They are capable, at least in a certain degree, of commanding their own thoughts; which command they find may be considerably increased by practice: or if their thoughts are not always the result of such command, they are naturally produced by the impression of external objects. Perhaps, "to make assurance doubly sure," they have purposely turned their thoughts from object to object, to prove that they were free. They can reason on any subject, form their designs, and put these designs in execution; they can rise or sit still; can move either the right or the left hand, at their own pleasure. How then, they ask, can they believe, that there is a divine power, reigning over these thoughts, designs, and actions, directing the whole, in such a manner as to secure a complete conformity to the purpose of God? They are sure of their own free agency; and because they cannot reconcile this doctrine with it, they reject the doctrine.

I believe in the free agency of man as firmly as they can do; but I do not believe this more firmly than I do that the eternal purpose of Jehovah, embracing the thoughts, designs, and actions of men, will take effect, at the precise moment to which it relates, with absolute certainty. Yet I neither comprehend, nor will I attempt to explain to you, the connexion between these two doctrines. Each of them is supported by its own appropriate evidence;

evidence fully sufficient to produce the most genuine conviction of its truth, in every candid mind. And surely we ought to believe every doctrine which is supported by sufficient evidence; for this is according to reason and Scripture; but to comprehend that doctrine is a very different thing. We believe that soul and body are united, but we do not comprehend this union; shall we on this account reject this belief? We believe that most of our bodily actions are the result of our own volition, but cannot explain the influence of the mind over the body; shall we therefore renounce our belief of the fact? In short, there is nothing which our limited minds can fully comprehend. We do not understand even that free agency of which we are conscious, still less can we comprehend the counsels of infinite wisdom. If then we can comprehend neither of these subjects, we cannot affirm that they are irreconcilable, or inconsistent with each other. In that part of their nature which is beyond the reach of our minds, and of which we can form no clear and definite conceptions, they may reign together and harmonize in perfect consistency. To affirm, as many do, that they cannot agree, presupposes, what no man ever possessed, a perfect comprehension of their nature. No man, I venture to say, would expose his own ignorance so far as to deny the prescience of God. This knowledge extends to all things; to every thought, word, and action of all mankind, to every event in the whole world; for " known unto God are all his works from the beginning;" " and all things are naked and opened unto the eyes of him, with whom we have to do." If one single thought were supposed to be unknown to him, from eternity, then his knowledge might be increased; but this it can-

THE DIVINE PURPOSE. 45

not be; for He is "perfect in knowledge." Here then is a case presenting the same difficulty which the other does; for it is just as impossible for us to comprehend the connexion between the foreknowledge of God, and the free agency of man, as between his decrees and this free agency: and yet no person denies the prescience of God on this account. The foreknowledge of God implies the absolute certainty of all events; yet no person ever supposed that it imposes any physical restraint, or necessity on the thoughts or actions of men; every one pursues that course to which his inclination leads him, as freely as if there was no prescience in the Deity. We find no difficulty in believing that divine justice and mercy are united, with perfect harmony, in the salvation of sinners through Jesus Christ; yet, in all probability, before the sublime and wonderful scheme was made known, angels considered this union impossible; because they could not comprehend it. The condemnation of a sinner would entirely exclude the exercise of mercy; his pardon would as effectually deny the claims of justice. How groundless and how presumptuous would have been the conclusion, that they could not be reconciled; and that, therefore, there was no such attribute as mercy belonging to Deity. Thanks be to God, we are taught, and so are the angels, to believe in this union; because it is demonstrated in the redemption of fallen man. So we now believe that, from all eternity, they were united; though the precious fact is only known through the cross of a divine Saviour. In a state of clearer vision, at some period of their endless progress in knowledge, the saints may yet comprehend the connexion between the high and holy purposes of God, and the free agency of intelligent creatures. This may be one grade of their boundless elevation; this may be part of the happiness reserved for them in heaven. With a devout expansion of thought, inconceivable to them at present, from some future exaltation, they may look back on the difficulties which now attend this subject, with the same feeling with which the man of science looks back on the faint, the dark, and imperfect conceptions of infancy and childhood.

It does not appear to me, that those act consistently who deny the doctrine respecting the divine decrees, because they cannot reconcile that doctrine with the free agency of man, when similar difficulties, in other cases, do not prevent their belief. If they believe in the union of soul and body, and in the influence of mind over body; if they believe in the prescience of God, and yet acknowledge that in each of these cases, there are difficulties which they cannot comprehend, why should they not also believe in the fore-ordination of God, though they cannot reconcile it, or rather cannot comprehend its reconciliation with the free agency of men? Especially when the truth of this doctrine is supported by authority as abundant, and as amply sufficient to produce conviction, as in either of the other cases. They, no doubt, and perhaps yourself also, will reply, let us have this authority. You shall have what I conceive amounts to such authority.

In the Bible many occurrences were foretold by the prophets long before they happened. These prophecies rendered the events to which they related undeniably certain; so much so, that they are often spoken of in the present tense, or as having already taken place; when in reality several hundred years were to intervene. In many instances where the prophecy was delivered, there appeared to human view little or no probability that it would ever be verified: still it was not the less certain; for it was the language of eternal and immutable truth. Its accomplishment often required the instrumentality of man, whose free agency is not to be suspended; still it is certain, " for the mouth of the Lord hath spoken it."

By the voice of prophecy God was pleased to make known to man various events which he intended to accomplish; one of which was the destruction of Babylon, and the subversion of the Chaldean empire. Isaiah appears to have been the first prophet by whom the divine purpose respecting this city was declared. It is found in the 13th chapter of his Prophecies, and is entitled, *The burden of Babylon*. This prediction is by chronologers, supposed to have been delivered about two hundred years before the event took place. In the judgment of human wisdom, many circumstances appeared to render this occurrence very improbable. The Jews were residing in quietness in their own land; and yet one design of this calamity was to release them from captivity; of which they had not at this time the least expectation. Indeed, it is supposed that the Jews had as yet but little acquaintance with the Chaldeans. The Medes, who are particularly mentioned as the executors of the divine decrees, were at this time but an inconsiderable people. Babylon for many years subsequent to this prophecy continued to increase in population, in opulence and power, until it reached its zenith, during the reign of Nebuchadnezzar, when it fully answered the description of the prophets, who called it " great Babylon; the beauty of the Chaldees' excellency; the golden city," &c. Yet powerful and splendid as it was, the prophet saw it, in the volume of the divine counsels, prostrate in ruin, swept with the besom of destruction.

The downfall of this proud metropolis of the east was predicted, not merely in general terms, but with considerable minuteness. The city was to be invaded; her monarch and her nobles slain; her treasures carried off; her once crowded population to be dispersed; wild beasts were to become her inhabitants; her walls, her palaces, and temples either demolished by the hand of man, or gradually consumed by the ravages of time; her very surface was destined to become a desert, no longer affording sustenance even to the wild beasts, which were then to be succeeded by serpents and scorpions, lurking beneath the fragments of her ruins, and threatening death to man; so that even the roving and adventurous Arab would be deterred from pitching his tent there.

The agents to be employed in fulfilling these prophecies were particularly mentioned. The Medes were named for this purpose; and for this reason the Lord calls them *his sanctified ones,* whom he had appointed and set apart for this service. About thirty years after, the commander-in-chief of these victorious armies is called by name, upwards of one hundred years before he was born. Cyrus is the man chosen to triumph over Babylon; and thus to commence the fulfilment of those prophecies relating to that devoted city. For this reason the Lord calls him *his anointed;* as one set apart and qualified for this work. His success was certain; for the King of kings promised to go before him, and hold his right hand.

Many circumstances respecting the manner in

which Cyrus would enter the city, are particularly mentioned. Babylon, when subjugated by the Medes, was surrounded by a wall, as historians inform us, *sixty miles* in compass, *eighty feet* thick, and *three hundred and fifty feet* high; forming an exact square, each side of which was *fifteen miles* long, built of brick, cemented with bitumen, which in a short time becomes harder than the brick. In each of the four sides were *twenty-five* gates, formed of solid brass, opening into the same number of streets which crossed each other at right angles. A branch of the river Euphrates passed through the city, dividing it into two equal parts. The banks of the river were faced with strong brick walls, to keep it within its channel, and were extended several miles beyond the city. Opposite to each street, on either side of the river, was a brazen gate in the wall, with stairs leading down from it to the river; which gates were open in the day and shut in the night. The river passing through the city was more than a quarter of a mile broad, and ten or twelve feet deep. It was explicitly foretold that this *river* should be *dried up;* also that these *two-leaved brazen gates* should be *opened* before Cyrus, and *not be shut*. It was predicted that the city should be taken by surprise, and during a drunken feast; and that the king should be instantaneously seized with the greatest horror and dismay. No time was yet specified for the accomplishment of these purposes. At length this also is given. Seventy years before these events actually commenced, the prophet was inspired to declare, that at the end of that period, the king of Babylon should be punished with these calamities. Jer. xxv. 12.

LETTER VI.

THE DIVINE PURPOSE PERFECTLY CONSISTENT WITH THE FREE AGENCY OF MAN.

The page of prophecy has informed us what God intended to do respecting Babylon; the same page in part, but chiefly the page of profane history, will inform us of the exact accomplishment of all these pre-ordinations. As the time approaches for the divine purpose to take effect, we see every agent and every circumstance mentioned in the prediction appearing, and assuming a state of preparation for the grand catastrophe. Evil-merodach, son and successor of Nebuchadnezzar, took one important step in that preparation, by making an unprovoked attack on the Medes. Neriglisser, his successor, hastens this preparation. Jealous of the growing power of the Medes, he excites against them a general confederacy of the neighbouring nations. Thus the Medes were fired with a spirit of irreconcilable enmity and revenge against Babylon. At the proper moment, the commander-in-chief of the invading army is born and is called Cyrus; a name given him by the prophet an hundred years before his birth. The first twelve years of his life were spent with his father; and he was educated after the Persian manner, in hardship and toil, and all such laborious exercises as would tend to fit him for the fatigues of war. At this early period, he surpassed all of his age, not only in his aptness to learn, but in the courage and address with which he executed whatever he undertook. The next five years were spent at the court of

Media, with his grandfather. Here he was generally beloved on account of his generous and amiable disposition, and especially for the military prowess which he displayed. He engaged particularly the affections of the king and the nobility, and thus laid the foundation for that attachment to his person which enabled him to act an important part in that great drama just opening on the world. He then returned to the Persian court, and resided with his father till he attained the age of forty. By this time so many preparatory events had taken place as pointed out the period for some decisive movement. The last sand, measuring the glory of Babylon, is now ready to fall. Accordingly Cyrus is appointed generalissimo of an army composed of Medes and Persians. This army approaches the devoted city; *for where the carcass is, there will the eagles be gathered together.* Belshazzar, who then reigned at Babylon, hearing that Cyrus was approaching his metropolis, marched out to give him battle: but being easily routed, he retreated into the city, where he was closely besieged. But the great height and strength of the walls, environed with ditches, and impregnable to every mode of attack then known; the numerous troops employed in their defence; immense magazines of provisions, sufficient for the consumption of many years, with the great extent of fertile land within the city, capable of furnishing continual supplies; all concurred in rendering the siege of Babylon an arduous and almost hopeless enterprise. This extraordinary combination of difficulties did not discourage Cyrus, nor did length of time overcome his perseverance. Despairing of taking the city by storm, he drew round its immense circuit a line of circumvallation, with a large and deep ditch, to cut off its communication with the country. But the Babylonians, trusting in the strength of their walls, their vast magazines and fruitful gardens, insulted Cyrus from the ramparts, and seemed to defy all his efforts, and thus resigned themselves to a fatal security. Cyrus, having spent two whole years before Babylon without making any impression, adopted the following stratagem, which proved successful. There was, on the west side of the city, a vast lake, dug to receive the waters of the river, while the brick walls which faced its banks were building, and also to receive the redundant waters in time of great floods, and thus to preserve the plain country from inundation. Informed that a great annual festival was about to be kept in the city, and that it was customary to spend the whole night on these occasions in drunkenness and debauchery, he determined to embrace this opportunity for surprising them. Accordingly he sent a strong detachment to the head of the great canal, leading from the river to the lake, with orders, at a particular hour, to break down the bank which separated between the lake and the canal, and thus to turn the whole current of the river into the lake. At the same time he stationed one body of troops where the river entered the city, and another below where it came out, with orders to march in by the bed of the river as soon as they should find it fordable. The same evening he caused the head of his trenches on both sides of the river above the city to be cut, that the water might discharge itself into them; so that by means of these different outlets, the channel was soon low enough to admit the entrance of the troops. The two bodies of troops above mentioned, conducted by Babylonian desert-

THE DIVINE PURPOSE. 53

ers, entered by the bed of the river, and finding the brazen gates at the end of the streets left open in consequence of the riot and disorder of the night, they penetrated into the heart of the city without opposition. According to the concerted plan of operation, they met at the royal palace, where the king was giving a grand licentious entertainment to *a thousand of his nobles.* Dan. v. 1. The supposition of some writers, that these troops had already entered the city, when *the hand-writing appeared on the wall,* is extremely probable. Having surprised and cut off the guards, they rushed into the palace and slew the king and his dissolute courtiers. The people being apprized of this event, submitted, and the victory was complete without further opposition. The reduction of Babylon put an end to the Babylonian empire, and finally fulfilled in the name and character of the conqueror, and in the various circumstances which attended this event, the prophecies which Isaiah, Jeremiah, and Daniel had uttered against this proud metropolis.

Here we may remark with what accuracy the predictions of the prophets were verified in this victory, and in the consequences which flowed from it. While the prophecies are receiving their accomplishment, there is no violence done to the free agency of man; and yet men are the principal agents in producing these effects. Every person concerned is influenced, in the ordinary way, by the circumstances with which he was surrounded. It is highly probable, if not certain, that Cyrus knew nothing of these prophecies, and of course could not act with a design to fulfil them; and yet had this been the fact, had he been acquainted with them from his youth, and had he intended their accomplishment, he could not possibly have done it more accurately than he did. His parents gave him the very name mentioned by the prophet Isaiah, an hundred years before he was born. He received precisely that education, possessed that temper of mind, and that constitution of body, which qualified him to act the part assigned him. He grew up with an increasing thirst for military fame, without which he would not have undertaken, or been fitted for the enterprise. Every circumstance attended, every event occurred, at the proper moment necessary to verify the emphatic language of the prophet, " I girded thee." The girding implies all that was requisite to fit him for this memorable campaign. The martial spirit which he by nature possessed; the active employments, the toils and fatigues in which he was from his infancy trained; that noble disposition, and those pleasing manners, by which he gained the favour and confidence of the kings and nobles both of Persia and Media, were all essential parts of this preparation. Had he possessed a timid spirit, had his disposition been grovelling and mean, his manners uncouth and forbidding, he would not have been girded for this purpose. Without the lake, into which Cyrus turned the waters of the Euphrates, he could not have gained the victory; because there was no other way in which he could enter the city. This lake, intended by those who dug it for a very different purpose, was designed by Providence to enable Cyrus to dry up the river, and thus to enter. Had the brazen gates, placed at the end of the streets leading to the river, been securely shut, he could not, even from the river, have entered the city or reached the palace. But this was one circumstance particularly mentioned by the prophet;

"I will loose the loins of kings, to open before him the two-leaved gates, and the gates shall not be shut." Isaiah xlv. 1. We are informed that it was the constant practice to close these gates every night, yet on this night they were not shut.

Other kings, and other causes, through successive ages, have contributed to the complete accomplishment of all the particulars, predicted by the prophets, respecting the ruin of the splendid city. At this day, the place where it stood cannot with certainty be ascertained.

Nothing can be more undeniably certain than that God had determined the capture and desolation of Babylon long before the event took place; for the prophets were inspired to announce this determination to the world. This determination must necessarily include and secure the existence and co-operation of all the agents, means, and circumstances on which the event depended. Had one of these agents been wanting, one of these causes failed to operate, one of these circumstances been different, the event, without a miracle, would not have taken place. God, however, who decreed the event, decreed also the means necessary for the accomplishment of his purpose.

Men were the principal agents in executing the divine plan. Cyrus was his anointed; the Medes were his sanctified ones; the loins of the kings of Babylon were loosed. These men were all free agents, who willingly performed their respective parts, without being conscious of the slightest compulsion. They knew not the Lord, nor his designs. Of Cyrus particularly, one of the principal agents, it is affirmed, that he knew him not. Their thoughts were employed as freely about the objects which engaged their attention as ours are.

They deliberated, formed their own plans, provided their means, selected their own time, and proceeded to bring these means into operation, for the execution of these plans according to their own intentions and views of propriety. And yet all this was perfectly according to the fore-ordination of God respecting Babylon. Every object which interested their attention, the dispositions and passions by which they were impelled, the means they provided, the time they selected, the plans they formed, the end they proposed, were all subservient to the designs of Jehovah, and contributed with perfect accuracy to the execution of his plans. Had no such purpose existed in the divine mind, they could not have deliberated and acted with greater freedom than they did; and yet had they been as destitute of reason and free agency as the hail, snow, or stormy wind, they could not better have fulfilled the word of God, or better answered his purpose.

We have, then, as it appears to me, the very best authority for believing that the divine purposes are accomplished with absolute certainty, through the agency of men, while these men think, deliberate, and act, with the greatest freedom. Their free agency is not suspended; nor does it, for a moment, suffer the least violence. No man can deny either of these propositions without involving himself in contradiction and absurdity. Both are undeniably true; and, therefore, do not imply the least inconsistency; for truth is always consistent. But while this is my firm belief, I repeat that I cannot comprehend this consistency. Neither can I comprehend the manner of the divine operations in any case, or on any subject. How the universe was created, how it is sustained and governed, I cannot comprehend; and yet, if I believe any thing, I believe that it was created, that it is sustained and governed by the wisdom and power of God. I cannot comprehend the influence of my own mind on my body; and yet the pen which writes these words, is moving in consequence of that influence.

LETTER VII.

A METHOD OF ASCERTAINING THE EXTENT OF DIVINE PROVIDENCE—GREAT EVENTS NATURALLY INCLUDE ALL THE LESS ONES, OF WHICH THEY ARE MADE UP.

You will admit, no doubt, that the subjugation of Babylon was decreed by the Ruler of the universe, long before the event took place; for so it was predicted by the prophets. Now, this is the nature of all prophecy: certain parts of the divine plan, according to the counsels of his own wisdom, respecting nations, cities, or individuals are made known to man. As soon as the prophecy is delivered, the decree of God is thus known. Many of these prophecies have been, others still remain to be fulfilled. Of those which have been accomplished, relating to cities, none are more remarkable than those respecting Jerusalem, delivered by our Saviour. Josephus records the exact and dreadful accomplishment of these predictions. Of those relating to individuals, none are more remarkable than those which foretold the birth, the life, the character, the sufferings, and death of Jesus Christ; the accomplishment of all which, even to the minutest circumstance, is contained in the New Testament. I need not tell you that the

Bible, from the beginning to the end, is filled with prophecies; all of which are declarations from God, making known to man, his intentions and purposes.

That these purposes existed in the divine mind, before they were communicated to the prophet, is undeniable. It is equally undeniable in my view, that they existed from all eternity. To suppose any thing else, is to make God imperfect and mutable like ourselves. As our knowledge increases, and our views enlarge, we form new plans, propose new ends. Not so, however, with God. His knowledge and wisdom are infinite, and can receive no addition; and his purposes are as eternal as his wisdom; the reasons on which they were founded always existed. There never was a period, in time or eternity, if the expression be allowed, when the purposes relating to Babylon and Jerusalem did not exist in the divine mind; and exist, too, in all that detail, in which they were made known through the prophets, and have long since been verified in the history of those cities. This may be affirmed of all the prophecies contained in the Bible; from all eternity, it was the unalterable purpose of God, that all those events should take place which the prophets had predicted.

Although, I doubt not, but you read the Bible with care and profit, yet let me request you to read it for the special purpose of ascertaining all the prophecies which it contains, from the first to the last. Note down, in one column, those which relate to nations, including all their population; in another, those relating to cities, with their inhabitants; in another, those respecting individuals, &c. In connexion with each of these, as far as practicable, note the events predicted. Then go somewhat more into detail; consider all the agents, with their qualifications; all the means, with their operation; the existence of all the circumstances, indispensably necessary to the occurrence of these events. From a review of the whole, although you may not be convinced that "all things, whatsoever come to pass," are embraced, yet, I rather think, you will be surprised to find what a great number, and vast variety of events will be included in this plan; all of which were, of course, embraced in the purpose of God, and thus rendered certain.

The promises of God, especially those called unconditional promises, are of the same nature; the fulfilment of them is undeniably certain. All the agents, means, and circumstances, necessary for their fulfilment, are equally certain. Such was the promise of God, to Abraham, respecting Ishmael: "Of the son of the bond-woman will I make a nation, because he is thy seed." Gen. xxi. 13. Go through your Bible a second time, and note all such promises; consider all the agents, means, and circumstances implied in verifying these words of the Lord, and you will find it will very much increase the number and variety of those events, thus rendered certain, long before they take place. These promises, like the prophecies, rest on the faithfulness of God, which cannot fail; his character is pledged for the accomplishment of both.

Note also, all those events, which although neither predicted nor promised, are yet explicitly ascribed to God; such as the preservation of human life, feeding the ravens, clothing the grass, &c., consider all the means and second causes on which these events depend. All these works of the Lord are performed according to an intention previously existing in the Divine mind; which intention secures the occurrence of the events, with all the second causes on which they depend. After casting your eye over the whole scheme, thus arranged, permit me to ask you, what event is there, belonging to this world, which is not included, either in the prophecies, the promises, or the works plainly ascribed to God? Nor can I perceive the least exaggeration, or unfairness in this process, which you may pursue with both pleasure and profit; the whole of it rests on the firm basis of Scripture, which cannot be shaken.

Some, I am aware, will readily admit that certain great events, such as the capture of Babylon, and the destruction of Jerusalem, were fore-ordained, in the counsels of eternal wisdom, but they hesitate in admitting all the details, without which these events could not take place. In my view, however, the latter are necessarily implied and embraced in the former. Babylon is to fall; not by an earthquake, nor by the lightning of heaven; but by an army of men. This army must have a commander; the existence, therefore, of this commander is certain; equally certain is the existence of his parents before him; these also were born of parents, who preceded them, and so on through all the line of their ancestors up to Noah, and from Noah to Adam, who came immediately from the hand of God. But this commander, distinguished as he was for military powers, could not have achieved the victory alone: an army was necessary. This army was composed of individuals; of course, the existence of these individuals was certain; for without them there could be no army; and without an army, Babylon could not be taken; and thus the prophecy could not have been fulfilled. Two-leaved gates were to be opened before Cyrus. Will any person venture to say that this does not render certain the existence of such gates? Yet these gates were formed by men who were influenced by their own motives, and without the least knowledge of the purpose of God. In the same manner they were left open. Similar remarks may be made respecting the destruction of Jerusalem. This devoted city was to be surrounded and destroyed by an army; this army must have a commander; this rendered certain, therefore, the existence both of the commander, and of the individuals who composed that army.

Many prophecies in the Old Testament relate exclusively to the divine Saviour. He was to be a descendant of David. Does not this necessarily secure the existence of some, at least, of David's descendants until this wonderful child should be born? The place of his birth is mentioned. But Bethlehem is not the residence of his parents. Their presence there, however, at the appointed time, is rendered certain by the prediction. I need not mention to you, the reasons which induced them to visit this village. In short, how often do the Evangelists, in narrating the events of his life and of his death remark, " This was done that it might be fulfilled which was spoken by the prophet."

It has already appeared what an extensive influence, over the world of nature, divine providence must employ in preserving the life of one individual: the promise of God, that he would make of Ishmael a nation, was made with a perfect knowledge of all that was necessary to secure its accomplishment, and with a real intention to provide all the means necessary for that purpose. Ishmael of course was preserved through many dangers, and from him has descended a nation which exists to this day. This is only one of a great number of promises, involving a divine control over a vast variety of events, all of which were necessary to the fulfilment of these promises, and the occurrence of which was unalterably fixed.

To admit that some great events are decreed, and thus rendered certain, and yet not to admit, in like manner, that all the details, all the particular parts, on which the great event depends, manifests, it appears to me, a want of reflection, an ignorance of the Bible, and of the character and providence of God, with which no consistent and intelligent Christian should be chargeable. The truth is, that all great events are made up of smaller ones combined together. That purpose of God which renders certain the occurrence of great events, renders equally certain, in their own time and order, the occurrence of all those smaller events, of which the great one is made up. The ocean is made up of single drops; the earth is composed of small atoms. Without drops, there could be no ocean; without atoms, no earth. To suppose that God determined to create the earth, without determining to create the atoms of which it is composed, is not more inconsistent with truth, or more unworthy the wisdom and character of God, than to suppose that he determined the occurrence of a great event, without including in his determination, all the subordinate events, even down to the minutest circumstance, on which the great one depends. The conquest of Babylon was a great event. This was gained by an army composed of individuals, whose concurrent and united exertions resulted in this conquest. Without a certain degree of muscular strength and military skill, these exertions could not have been made; without regular and suitable nourishment, this strength could not be secured; without previous training, this skill could not be acquired. Had this training, and this nourishment not been received, this strength and this skill would not have been possessed; of course, these exertions could not have been made; without these, the victory could not have been gained; and thus the divine prediction would have failed; the word of the Lord would have returned to him void.

The man who makes a promise to his neighbour, without having in view the probable means of fulfilling it, is chargeable with imprudence, dishonesty, or wickedness, perhaps all together. If your neighbour, labouring under pecuniary embarrassments, should apply to you for the loan of a particular sum which would relieve him, and promise to repay it at the end of twelve months, you would no doubt wish to be informed of the means that would secure a compliance with his promise. If he could satisfy you on this point, you would consider this promise reasonable, and grant him relief. But if he failed in giving this satisfaction; if he possessed no probable means of complying with his promise; you would not only refuse to trust him, but would consider him a dishonest man, who intended to deceive you. Let us beware, then, of ascribing to God our Maker, a procedure which would disgrace a human being, even in the view of such sinful creatures as we are. Let God be true, though every man should be a liar. When he promises the occurrence of any event or state of things, it is with an immutable intention of accomplishing that promise. The means of this accomplishment are as distinctly in his view, and as much the objects of his care, and the subjects of his control, as the event itself. Suppose him to leave these out of view, or to possess no power to secure their existence, and you suppose him to resemble a weak and imprudent man.

Long before the event occurred, the prophets declared the intention of God, that Babylon should be taken. This intention, as we have seen, existed in the divine mind from all eternity. But unless Babylon exists it cannot be taken. This intention, therefore, rendered unalterably certain, before the foundation of the world, the existence of Babylon. When the earth received its form, the site of this city was marked out on its surface. This spot, destined to be the theatre of such memorable events, may, through successive ages, be covered by the trees of the forest, may be the resort of wild beasts, be untrodden by the foot of man; but at the appointed hour the forest shall disappear, the wild beasts shall seek another resort, the architect shall stretch his line and execute his plans—here the walls shall run, here the temple and the palace shall stand, and Babylon shall rear her head to the skies. When or by whom this city was founded is uncertain. "Some say it was founded by Semiramis, and according to others by Belus, who is thought by many to be the same with Nimrod; but whoever was the founder, it was, in process of time, much improved; and Nebuchadnezzar in particular repaired, enlarged, and beautified it to such a degree, that he may be said to have built it according to his own vain-glorious boast: 'Is not this great Babylon, which I have built for the house of the kingdom, by the might of my power, and for the honour of my majesty?'" Dan. iv. 30. Babylon is not only to exist, but to exist in a style of splendour that would verify the descriptive language of Scripture respecting it. It is there represented as "great Babylon—the golden city—the lady of kingdoms—abundant in treasures—the praise of the whole earth." Profane historians inform us that such was the extent, the strength, the wealth and splendour of Babylon, as to answer these prophetic descriptions: it was for ages considered one of the wonders of the world. Now, unless Babylon exists, it cannot be taken; unless it is built, it cannot exist; it was not built by miracle, but by human agents, by men; these men were rational, were free agents like ourselves. They would not have acted their respective parts without motives, leading them to act; these motives must have been derived from their own dispositions, and the circumstances in which they were placed. Had these dispositions and these circumstances been different, these motives would not have existed; without them, these men would not have acted; without their agency, the city could not have been built; of course could not have been taken; by consequence, the prophets who foretold this event, would have been found false prophets. But they were not false, but true prophets. The divine purpose which they were commissioned to reveal, secured the existence of the city; of course, rendered certain the existence of every agent, circumstance and motive, in their proper time and degree, necessary to complete his designs. These men, marked out by divine wisdom for these purposes, knew not the Lord nor his intentions. Nebuchadnezzar knew not that the Most High ruled in the kingdom of men. He tells us what was his object, in all that he did: "Is not this great Babylon, which I have built for the honour of my majesty?" He laid his own plans, proposed his own ends; yet over these plans and these ends, the high purposes of Jehovah reigned with perfect ease and certainty, rendering them subservient to the existence and unparalleled magnificence of this renowned city, as it was found and conquered by Cyrus.

LETTER VIII.

EVENTS, SIMILAR TO THOSE CONTAINED IN THE PROPHECIES AND PROMISES OF GOD, ARE ALL INCLUDED IN HIS PURPOSE.

Is your patience so far exhausted, or is your mind so well satisfied, that you wish for nothing more on this subject? I wish to offer a few additional remarks; you can read or omit them as you think proper.

It was the intention of God that Babylon should exist, and that it should be captured by Cyrus. For purposes of his own glory, he was pleased to make known this intention to the world long before the events occurred. These events did not occur because this revelation was made, though in perfect accordance with it. The design existed before the revelation was made. The occurrence of these events was not in the least degree more certain after this revelation than they were before. It was the intention of God, and not the communication of that intention to man which rendered certain this great series of events. If it had been according to the counsels of his wisdom, to have withheld from man all knowledge of this intention, these events would have taken place precisely at the time and in the same order in which they did. Our ignorance of the divine purpose can neither alter the nature, nor hasten or retard the accomplishment of that purpose. After the events had taken place, we might then have been as certain that they were embraced in the divine plan, as if they had been predicted by the prophets. Hence, according to my view, we are authorized to infer, that all events similar to those that have been foretold, and similar to those which God has promised to accomplish, are equally embraced in the divine purpose, with those which he has revealed to man. We infer this, not from prophecies or promises, but from the occurrence of the events themselves. Whatever is accomplished by the agency of God, is accomplished according to an intention, previously existing in his mind; our knowledge, or our ignorance of this intention, can have no influence on its execution. The Jews, at least the prophets, knew that Babylon was to be taken; yet we do not find that they had any agency in bringing the event to pass: Cyrus was ignorant of the divine intention, and yet accomplished the will of God. Suppose there had lived a pious Jew, who had never seen the predictions respecting the capture of Babylon, but who had witnessed the occurrence of the event, might he not, with the greatest certainty, from his knowledge of the divine character and government, have inferred, that such had been the intention of God from all eternity? If these very prophecies had been afterwards submitted to his inspection, it could not have increased the certainty of his conclusion. With equal certainty we may infer that all similar events, accomplished in the providence of God, were fixed before the foundation of the world, in his wise and holy purpose.

The existence, the magnificence, and downfall of Babylon, were predicted; this prediction was the divine intention made known to man. In the book of God, no prediction is found respecting London, Paris, New York, or Philadelphia. We know however, that these cities do exist. Their rise, progress, and present state, were all determined in the divine purpose; for similar circumstances were thus determined respecting Babylon. From all eternity, it was as certain that these modern cities should exist in their present state, as that the famed metropolis of the east should exist in the state in which Cyrus found it. What the future destiny of these cities is to be, we cannot tell; the purpose of God respecting them is not made known to us. Our ignorance, however, cannot alter it, in the least. That purpose as certainly exists, and will as certainly take effect, as if we knew it in all its details. Whether they shall remain to feed the flames of the general conflagration, or be demolished by an earthquake, or moulder under the ravages of time, or be razed from their foundations by some victorious enemy, we cannot tell; it is known, however, to God as distinctly as it will be at the last moment of time; and the progress of divine providence will disclose it to the world. The same remarks may be made, with equal truth, respecting every city, town or village, which ever has existed, which does now, or ever shall exist on this earth. Their beginning, their progress, and their end, were all fixed in the counsels of Him who views, with one intuitive glance, the past, the present, and what is to come.

It is but a few years ago when Moscow, one of the ancient cities of Russia, became the theatre of events which filled the civilized world with astonishment. A mighty chief, the late emperor of France, with his victorious army, approached its walls. The governor formed and executed the desperate resolution of laying the city in ashes, and thus leaving the enemy nothing but a mass of smouldering ruins to shelter them from the inclemencies of winter. The flight of that chief, and the almost unparalleled sufferings and carnage of his army, soon followed as the result of that daring measure of defence. Now, in my opinion, there are sufficient reasons to believe that this whole series of events was predetermined, from the beginning of the world, in the divine plan; and that this plan embraced all the agents and causes, and even the minutest circumstances which in any manner or degree contributed to the grand result.

Still more recently, a series of events occurred, more deeply interesting to our feelings than even the flames of Moscow. During the late war, the enemy invaded the metropolis of our beloved country, and laid our capitol and other public buildings in ashes. Shall we suppose that these events were not embraced in the purpose of Him who ruleth among the nations? Or did they happen unexpectedly to him? Was it not the hand of Providence that guided the march of General Ross, as well as the march of Cyrus? It will, perhaps, be replied, that he was prompted by his own ambition. This is readily admitted; and yet the admission does not in the least affect the conclusion, that this whole transaction, with all its details, was embraced in the divine determination. Cyrus, in his operations against Babylon, was prompted by his own motives; and yet his motives, with the conduct to which they led, were the very means of accomplishing the purposes of God. General

Ross could not have been influenced by his own intentions, nor have acted as a free agent more than Cyrus did; and yet Cyrus "executed the counsel, and performed all the pleasure of the Lord." For this purpose the Lord "girded him, went before him, directed all his ways, and held his right hand." To my mind, there can be no reasons for supposing that General Ross, with his limited and momentary victory, was not as certainly and as distinctly embraced in the divine purpose, as Cyrus and his victory were. The only difference is this: the name, character, and conquest of Cyrus had been predicted; no prophet had given similar information respecting General Ross and his operations. And yet had this been the fact; had it pleased God, two hundred years ago, to make known that a man by the name of Ross, at the head of an army, should come from the kingdom of Great Britain, and in the year 1814, in the month of August, enter the city of Washington in triumph, burn the capitol and other public buildings, and then hastily retire; this revelation would not have rendered the events in the least more certain than they were. From the time of such revelation down to the hour when the smoke of the buildings ascended, those who had access to that revelation, might have known that such an event would certainly take place. Had we known that this occurrence was fixed in the purpose of the Almighty, our exertions could not have prevented it. The prophecies of God have often been accomplished by those who knew nothing of them; and generally, I believe, by those who, whether they knew them or not, had no such intention at the time. No efforts made with a design to frustrate them can ever be successful. The mighty hand that rolls along the dispensations of Providence, will crush the impious wretch who dares to make opposition. "My word shall not return to me void; I will do all my pleasure, saith the Lord."

If it was certain from the beginning, that Moscow should become a heap of ruins, then it was equally certain that Moscow should be built, and remain till the very hour when the torch was applied to it. This secured the existence and exertions of those who built and preserved it. The city of Washington was to be invaded, and must, therefore, exist. But its existence was impossible without the agency of men, under the influence of such motives as led to this result. These agents, and their motives, together with the circumstances from which they were derived, were all guided and limited in their operations by the divine purpose. But why was Moscow laid in ashes? Nothing but the most urgent necessity could have dictated such a measure. A powerful enemy approached; the flames were to snatch the city from his grasp; and deprive him of the comfort which its provisions and its palaces might afford. Without this necessity, this fire would not have been kindled; without the approach of such an enemy, this necessity would not have existed; the counsels of infinite wisdom, therefore, which determined that Moscow should be burnt, determined all the circumstances also which led to this catastrophe—that a man, impelled by boundless ambition, commanding a numerous and victorious army, should approach the city; also, as the result has proved, that these ruins should be the barrier to his success, should, like the shores of the ocean, beat back the tide of his ambitious projects, and occasion the ebbing of his glory to commence. In like manner, the capitol of our country was not consumed by a friend; the hand of an enemy alone could perform a deed like this. The same unalterable counsel which determined the conflagration of that distinguished building, determined to provide a hand prepared for the task. From the moment of his birth, from the foundation of the world, this was to be the work of General Ross; none could deprive him of the distinction which he gained by its performance.

Might it not be a pleasing and edifying employment of your leisure hours to meditate on the designs of Jehovah respecting the American continent, and especially respecting these United States, designs which are eternal as the mind in which they exist? The knowledge of them is not obtained from prophetic records, but from the page of history, and from observation; not from inspiration, but from the occurrence of those events, embraced in these designs. Passing over those successive centuries, during which the very existence of this country was unknown to Europe, begin with Columbus, in the deliberations and conclusions of whose masterly genius, and in the execution of whose plans, the divine purpose began to develope itself. The steps taken in consequence of his important discoveries, furnish a still further development of that purpose. Come down to the period when the first permanent settlements were made on these shores. Think of all the causes which induced the first emigrants to leave their native country, and plant themselves in the new world. When this handful of men first set foot on the banks of the James River, what man, or angel, without the inspiration of God, would have predicted that this was the beginning of a mighty empire? Trace them through all their hardships and their perils; consider the annual accessions which they received from the mother country, till you come to the causes of the revolution. This is an epoch requiring a more than usual pause. What an enlargement have your views of the divine purpose now acquired? Over what a varied and interesting chain of events have you now passed, giving birth to a new series, not less varied, and if possible, still more important? If, just now, you contemplated this empire in its small beginning, in the wilds of Virginia; now you must search for the liberty and independence of the United States in the bosom of a few individuals. Perhaps in the mind of some one individual the thought first occurred, which under the fostering care of Providence, has matured into that noble tree, under the wide spread branches of which this empire now reposes. Enter the legislative hall, and listen to the grave and animated debates of our fathers involving liberty or death; hover over the field of battle, and with the sympathies of a brother, listen to the groans of the wounded and the dying; station yourself on the plains of Little York, and witness with exultation, the last scene of this bloody and protracted drama; with thankfulness to the Lord of hosts, hear the proclamation of peace and independence; see this land of freedom assuming a dignified rank among the nations of this earth. From that memorable era down to the present day you descend and dwell with grateful delight on the varied and multiplied blessings now enjoyed by these United States. These blessings you can easily trace back to the conclusions and discoveries of Columbus, through a chain of events which we must contemplate in detached parts, a link at a time, but which, as it is viewed, and as it exists in the divine mind, is one unbroken whole. Little did Columbus know the consequences which were to flow from the first faint and obscure conceptions of his mind. In the purpose of God, however, they were then as certain as they are now. In the counsels of his eternal wisdom, neither more nor less was intended than has been accomplished in his providence.

LETTER IX.

THE PURPOSES OF GOD NOT INCONSISTENT WITH THE MORAL AGENCY OF MAN.

I TRUST it has been made to appear that men who were employed in accomplishing the purposes of God, were free agents; and that therefore there is no inconsistency between them: the divine decree neither destroys nor suspends the free agency of man. Against this doctrine, however, what is considered a more serious objection, is sometimes urged; that it is inconsistent with the *moral agency* of man. If, according to the purpose of God, a man is to act a particular part, pursue a certain course of conduct, is he, or can he be, accountable for his conduct? or can he be criminal in acting this part? This objection merits and shall receive consideration.

In my own view, the free agency, and the moral agency of man, are substantially the same, and may be used as synonymous terms: what is generally called reason is the basis of both. When reason is wanting, neither free agency, nor moral agency can be predicated of any creature. According to the general opinion, brutes do not possess the faculty of reason; what they do is the result of instinct, not of free agency; of course they are not supposed to be moral agents, or to be accountable for their conduct. When it pleases God to deprive a man of his reason—a case which often occurs—we no longer consider him a moral agent. If he should even take the life of a fellow creature, the laws of our country do not consider him worthy of punishment. His conclusions and his conduct are the result of necessity; that is, of morbid impressions, made, as is generally believed, on his animal system. These conclusions, sometimes so disastrous in their consequences, govern his conduct; the shattered remains of reason being too feeble to correct or counteract them. If then the free agency and the moral agency of man are substantially the same, every argument which proves the consistency of the divine purposes with the free agency, proves with equal force and clearness, their consistency with the moral agency of man. For the purpose of proving and illustrating this consistency, the case of Cyrus, out of many others, equally pertinent, contained in the Bible, has been adduced. Profane historians inform us that in all his operations, he was influenced by his own motives, formed his plans, provided his means, pursued his ends, and in all respects, manifested a free agency as perfect as can be possessed or exercised by man. The Bible declares that he executed the counsel, and performed all the pleasure of God. The man, therefore, who can deny, or even doubt this consistency, can deny and doubt declarations of the Bible as explicit and unequivocal as it is possible for words to be. With such a man, it is vain to think of reasoning. If, while Cyrus was executing the counsel, and performing the pleasure of the Almighty, he remained a free agent, he was also a moral agent; for they are substantially the same. That which may, according to the Scripture, be affirmed of Cyrus, may, with equal truth, be affirmed of every other man whose agency has been, or ever shall be, employed in fulfilling the prophecies, or accomplishing the purposes of God. If the objection now under consideration, is removed; if it can be proved to have no weight in the case of one man, it is removed, and proved to have no weight in the case of every other man. If one has accomplished the designs of Jehovah and yet retained his moral agency, so may, and so does every son and daughter of Adam. God is no respecter of persons; as it regards their moral agency, they are all alike.

Cyrus was two whole years before the walls of Babylon before his efforts were crowned with success. During this time the prophecies and purposes of God were accomplished through his agency. When he stands before the judgment seat of Christ, will this period be omitted? will the thoughts, intentions, and conduct of these two years be left out of the account, and not appear in the books then to be opened? I think the most determined opponent of the doctrine which I defend, would not hazard an assertion to this effect. If, then, these years will not be omitted; if his thoughts, intentions, and conduct will appear, it unavoidably follows that, during this period, he was a moral agent; that he was accountable for those thoughts and that conduct which, with perfect accuracy, accomplished the divine purpose. If we have the highest authority for believing this respecting Cyrus, we have the same authority for believing it respecting every other human being.

Those who advance the objection above stated, conceive it difficult and even impossible to believe that God should determine to employ the agency of wicked men in fulfilling his designs. They seem to suppose this implies his approbation of that conduct, or at least furnishes some excuse for their wickedness. While I feel the most affectionate concern for pious Christians perplexed with scruples and difficulties, I cannot but suppose they have passed over many passages of the Bible without due consideration. Whatever is contained in the records of truth, we are bound to believe, whether we can comprehend its consistency and connexion with other parts or not. If I mistake not, there are many passages which show most clearly that such is the fact; that the wicked actions of man have fulfilled the purpose of divine providence.

The conduct of Joseph's brethren towards him was unquestionably cruel and very wicked; such they themselves acknowledged it to be, when the hand of adversity was pressing upon them. When cast into prison they say, " We are verily guilty concerning our brother; behold, said Reuben, his blood is required." Hear the language of Joseph, when he discovered himself to them, respecting this conduct: " Now therefore be not grieved, nor angry with yourselves that ye sold me hither; for God did send me before you to preserve life. God sent me before you to preserve you a posterity in the earth, and to save your lives by a great deliverance. So now it was not you sent me hither, but God." Gen. xlv. 5, 7. Here Joseph ascribes his being brought to Egypt, in the most explicit language, to God. If his brethren had done nothing in this business, if he had been caught up and conveyed by miraculous power, through the air, his language could not be more plain and forcible. We cannot avoid the conclusion, that he was sent into Egypt according to the purposes of God; and yet his brethren were the agents in sending him there. That they were not highly criminal in doing so, no man will pretend to affirm. Here, then, is a plain instance in which the designs of providence were accomplished by the wicked actions of men, without the slightest approbation of God to their conduct, or any excuse for their criminality.

The cursing of Shimei against David was no doubt sinful; yet David will not permit his friends to revenge the insult. "Let him curse, said the king, because the Lord hath said unto him, Curse David; let him alone, and let him curse; for the Lord hath bidden him." 2 Sam. xvi. 10, 11. David does not mean that the Lord approved of this cursing: but that it was a part of the affliction, appointed for him, during this hour of banishment and sorrow.

The death of Jesus Christ is a remarkable instance of this kind. None will deny that this event was fixed, was absolutely certain, in the counsels of infinite wisdom from all eternity. If ever the wisdom of Deity proposed an end worthy of a high and holy decree, it was this; that a Saviour should die. The first penitent sinner was pardoned and accepted of God, on the ground of this certainty. Thousands and tens of thousands were accepted on the same ground. The atonement, except in the divine purpose, was not yet made; but sinners were forgiven, which they could not have been without an absolute certainty that the great sacrifice for sin, would, at the appointed time, be offered up. They could not have been forgiven on uncertainty. The slightest uncertainty attaching to this subject would have shaken, would have blasted for ever their hopes of acceptance, and have thrown them back to the gulf of despair. Every sin that was pardoned, necessarily implied the certainty of this event. The pardon of sinners previous to the death of Christ, furnishes a view of this certainty, perhaps, better adapted than the divine decree to our comprehension. The Jewish sacrifices proclaimed the same truth. Every victim that bled at the altar pointed forward to the great antitype, one day to bleed for sin. The prophets announced to the world this merciful purpose of God. They dwell on the subject, in a variety of details which have more the appearance of history than of prophecy. They not only predict the death of the Saviour, but also the manner of that death. He was to die a violent death, under an unjust sentence, amidst the reproaches, calumnies, and derisions of men. That his blood should be shed, was just as certain as that he should die. This death was, therefore, certain in the divine purpose; this certainty was made known to the world, through the pardon of sinners, the Jewish sacrifices, and the predictions of the prophets. The New Testament contains the narrative of all these events; of all that was foretold by the prophets, prefigured by the Jewish types, implied in the pardon of sinners, and determined in the counsels of heaven. This purpose was executed by men, by his own countrymen, by the Jews, who annually witnessed the sacrifices bleeding at their altar, who had in their possession the prophecies, and heard them read every Sabbath-day. These were the men who, with malicious eyes, watched the conduct of the Saviour; who denied and rejected him; who extorted from Pilate, the sentence of his death; who purchased his blood; who apprehended and bound him; who nailed him to the cross, accompanying the whole with the most cruel abuse, insults, and mockeries. That in all this they accomplished the divine purpose, is, in my view, undeniable; that in all this they manifested a degree of wickedness, literally without a parallel, even in this guilty world, is also undeniable.

That they fulfilled the divine purpose, is if I mistake not, affirmed in explicit terms in Scripture—" Him being delivered by the determinate counsel and foreknowledge of God: For of a truth against thy holy child Jesus, whom thou hast anointed, both Herod and Pontius Pilate, with the Gentiles and the people of Israel, were gathered together, to do whatsoever thy hand and thy counsel determined before to be done." Acts ii. 23, and iv. 27, 28, also Acts iii. 18, and xiii. 27. Passages boldly and directly charging the Jews with the most diabolical wickedness in crucifying the Lord of glory, are numerous, and need not be quoted, especially as this point is undisputed. In all that they did, they were moral agents, and were as much accountable for their conduct as if no divine purpose had existed; and yet they fulfilled this counsel with as great accuracy as if they had not been moral agents. They were influenced entirely by their own motives. Their consultations, their stratagems and their plans, are often mentioned in the New Testament. I cannot, therefore, see how to avoid the conclusion, that the purpose of God is sometimes accomplished by wicked men, without furnishing the least excuse for that wickedness; and is not inconsistent with their moral agency.

If the purpose and providence of God have no control over the sinful thoughts, intentions, and conduct of men, then how great a portion of the human family are excluded from the wise and holy providence of Jehovah? All men are sinful by nature. In the judgment of Him who searcheth the heart, there is "none that doeth good; no, not one." Such have constituted a vast majority of the human race, in every past age of the world; at this day they are an overwhelming majority. This is the state and character of every pious man, till the moment of his conversion. When the finally impenitent transgressor shall stand before his Judge, not one thought, intention or desire of his heart, nor one single action of his life, will be pronounced good: all will be condemned as sinful and wicked. Those who advance the objection above to the doctrine for which I contend, cannot believe, if they will be consistent, that the wise and mighty Ruler of the universe can ever employ the agency of such men in the execution of his designs. He cannot employ their agency without controlling, in some way or other, their thoughts, intentions and conduct. But these are all sinful; he cannot therefore cause his holy determinations to be answered by any thing that is sinful; for this, according to their opinion, would imply his approbation of that sin, and be inconsistent with the moral agency of man. Hence, in their view, it is a fact, for which it behoves them to account, if they can, that none but sincerely pious men, and these only so far as they are pious, have ever been employed in promoting the dispensations of providence, or in executing the counsels of infinite wisdom, which is the same thing; and that no sinful man ever has, or ever will answer this purpose. Was Cyrus and his army; was Titus and his army, sincerely pious? The brethren who oppose us on this subject, must either maintain that they were, or deny that they ever fulfilled the prophecies, or executed the counsel of God. If they will do neither of these, their objection has no weight, even in their own view; and they ought, for the sake of consistency, to admit that the purposes of God are sometimes answered by sinful men; and that these purposes are not inconsistent with moral agency.

Affliction, we are told, "cometh not forth of the dust; neither doth trouble spring out of the ground." Afflictions are uniformly considered, in Scripture, as dispensations of Providence, sent for our improvement; that we may be partakers of his holiness. " They work together for good, to those who love God; they work out for us a far more exceeding and eternal weight of glory" than we could ever attain without them. But some of the heaviest afflictions we are ever called to bear, are occasioned by the wickedness of men. A pious father may witness the profligacy of a graceless son, or be called to weep over his untimely grave, to which he is brought by the hand of the duelist. An affectionate mother may have continually before her eyes a daughter, disgraced and ruined by the infernal art of some vile seducer. These are sore afflictions; severe trials. Are they sent for the good of those who are visited by them? Ought they to be improved in a religious manner? They were sent for good; and they ought to be improved. But who sent them? and who gave them a tendency to work for good, to produce the peaceful fruits of righteousness? Satan, if he had the power, has not the disposition to do any thing to promote the spiritual interest of men. Wicked men have neither the power nor disposition to do this. If they have a tendency to work for good, this must have been imparted to them by a being of infinite goodness, who designed and sent them for this purpose. Without this tendency, it cannot be a duty to improve them. But it is a duty to improve these and all other afflictions; and, therefore, they do possess this tendency. If they possess it, they must have derived it from God; for none else could impart it to them. If they were designed and sent by him, then his providence must extend to the cause from which they spring: and his purpose and his providence are co-extensive and co-eternal.

Hence we reach the same conclusion; that the purposes of God are not inconsistent with the moral agency of man; and that the control of his wise and holy providence is exercised over the wicked actions of men, without implying his approbation of that wickedness, or furnishing for it the least shadow of excuse.

LETTER X.

THIS CONSISTENCY INCOMPREHENSIBLE TO US—BUT SO ARE MANY OTHER THINGS WHICH YET WE BELIEVE.

Probably before this time you are anxious to propose the question of Nicodemus—" How can these things be?" Could you receive the answer from Him who taught Nicodemus, it would, no doubt, be satisfactory. Without claiming, or desiring to be any thing but an humble disciple at the feet of that teacher, may I not reply, in his language, adapted to this case—Art thou a student of the Bible, of the character and government of God, and knowest not these things? Do you not read of many undoubted instances of the divine purpose being accomplished through the agency of men, without in the least impairing or suspending their moral agency? If you find but even one such instance, this proves the fact and solves the difficulty. For if the determinations of God are consistent with the moral agency of man, in the case of one individual, they may be, and are consistent with the moral agency of all the human family. That Teacher has already given us all that he considered useful, and, therefore, all that is necessary, on the subject. This ought to satisfy every candid mind. When on earth, he never gratified the idle curiosity of any man; were he to converse again with men, he would act, no doubt, in the same manner.

The power of human language may be utterly insufficient to convey, to our minds, definite ideas any further than to teach the fact. This, I conceive is done, both in the Bible, and in the providence of God. The use of words which convey no definite ideas, is altogether vain. Our minds may be far too limited to comprehend this consistency. The attempt, therefore, to make us comprehend it would be fruitless: and God makes no fruitless attempts. If our capacities were sufficiently enlarged to grasp the magnitude of this subject, we should cease to be men; or if the subject was brought down to the present limits of our capacities, then it would cease to be the subject which it is. All that can be done is, to make us acquainted with so much, with such parts of the subject, as are comprehensible, and of course, useful to us. This, in my opinion, has been done. With this we ought to be satisfied; for this we ought to be grateful. That curiosity which pushes its inquiries further, is, in my opinion, of at least a suspicious character. We are not satisfied with the information which God has given us, unless it were extended further than divine wisdom has deemed proper and useful for us. We will not admit the existence of facts, unless we can comprehend the consistency and harmony of these facts. We will not receive truths suited to our own comprehension, unless we can receive those suited to superior intelligences: that is, unless we are raised to a higher grade in the scale of being. We will not be contented and thankful that we are men; we must be angels. Well, suppose we were elevated to the rank of angels: there are perfections in the character of Deity which even they cannot comprehend. " Can they by searching find out God? Can they find out the Almighty to perfection?" The same curiosity might lead them to desire capacities sufficiently enlarged to comprehend these perfections; that is, to be gods. If this curiosity were not gratified, they might be discontented; and all discontent of this kind is rebellion against the Most High. If it be wrong in them to indulge this curiosity, it must, at least, be suspicious in us. If they ought to be thankful for what they can comprehend of the works and character of God, so ought we; if they ought to be thankful and contented that they are angels, so ought we, that we are men.

I am far from charging with these consequences all who make this and similar inquiries; and because they do not receive answers, satisfactory to their view, reject the doctrine which I maintain: but I candidly think they have not duly considered the tendency of that curiosity, or of that spirit, from which this inquiry proceeds.

If, however, they will urge the inquiry; how can the purpose of God be consistent with the moral agency of men? I freely confess that I do not know: nor do I ever expect, in this life, to comprehend this subject. Men of greater research, of greater talents, and of much greater piety than I possess, have left the world, making the same confession. The man, therefore, who can seriously make the inquiry, must wait for the clearer light of futurity.

There are many other subjects respecting which the same inquiry might be made, to which the same confession of ignorance could only be given. How did God create the world? By his Almighty power, it might be answered. But should the inquirer renew the attack, and ask, how could divine power operate, when there was nothing to operate on, nothing on which this power could terminate? I confess as freely as in the other case, I do not know. How can, or how does God govern the world? I do not know. Shall we, therefore, refuse to believe that the world was created, and is governed by Jehovah? We may, it appears to me, just with the same consistency and truth with which we refuse to believe in the wise and holy purpose of God, according to which he created and governs the world.

THE DIVINE PURPOSE.

The love of Jesus Christ to guilty sinners, which surrounds the divine character with its brightest and mildest splendours, which animate the universe with new joys and new glories, is perfectly incomprehensible to us. Its height we cannot reach; its depth we cannot fathom; its length and breadth we cannot grasp. Of this love it is said with perfect truth, that it passeth knowledge. Thanks to the Divine Saviour! his love is infinitely greater than our comprehension. Shall we then ask, how can this love exist; or how can it be exercised? And until we have this difficulty removed; until it is brought down to our capacity, or our capacity is enlarged to its dimensions, shall we hesitate to rejoice in it? Because this explanation cannot be given; or if given, cannot be comprehended by us; shall we refuse to believe the reality of this love; that angels ever beheld and adored its exhibition; that the heart of a sinner ever felt its life-giving touch? shall we drive from our hearts the hopes which it inspires, and shut against ourselves the heaven to which it invites, and for which it prepares us? The man who would act thus would declare his own incorrigible wickedness, stamp his own character with the basest ingratitude, and fix on his own soul the seal of perdition. We have abundant evidence to support our belief in the reality and greatness of this love; yet this evidence does not render it comprehensible to us. The more we know of it, the more deeply are we convinced that it passeth our knowledge. Yet no man ever thought of alleging this as a reason why he would not receive and rejoice in it. Its greatness, on the contrary, is the ground of his joys and his hopes. Why we should not feel and act, in the same manner, respecting other truths of the Bible, I cannot tell.

That God is not the author of sin, I most firmly believe. Nothing in his character, in his word, or in his works, will justify such a belief. On the contrary, he declares that it is odious in his sight, and dangerous to us. As the righteous Governor of the universe he has most plainly, and positively, forbidden and condemned it; as our affectionate Father, he has warned us of its deceitful and ruinous tendency, and furnished us with the very strongest inducements to avoid it. And yet, that this is a sinful world, is a melancholy fact, which none, or very few at least, have been disposed to question. That we are sinners, is a plain proof that we are subjects of the moral government of God: for sin is a transgression of those laws, by which we ought to be governed. In the Bible those laws are contained, which show us what we ought to be. But the Bible is adapted to us as sinners; miserable, helpless sinners. Therefore, in addition to the moral law, it contains a revelation of mercy; a glorious plan of redemption, through the atoning blood of a crucified Saviour. It contains all that is necessary for us to know, in order to escape the consequences of sin, and regain the favour of God. That we are also under the government of divine providence is, in my opinion, as certain, as that we are under the moral government of God. That these two governments are perfectly consistent with each other is evident; because they are both conducted by the same wise, good, and almighty Being, whose perfections and designs perfectly harmonize. But although they are connected, and in harmony with each other, yet there is, in many respects, a difference. The government of providence is subservient to the moral government: the one is administered for the sake of the other. In proof of this it may be observed, that the laws of providence, or as they are generally called, the laws of nature, have frequently been suspended to promote the designs of the moral government; but no instance occurs of a moral law being suspended, to promote the designs of providence. The life of man is preserved by providence, that he may, as a moral agent, enjoy and glorify God. They differ also in this; none but intelligent creatures are subjects of the moral government; but all creatures, animate and inanimate, rational and irrational, are subject to the control of providence. They differ also in this; the laws of the moral government, as far, at least, as we are concerned, are fully made known; but the laws by which the government of providence is conducted, never have been, except in a few instances, made known to man. The exceptions to which I refer, are those events which have been predicted by the prophets, or secured in the promises of God. In both cases the laws of providence, respecting the events to which they relate, were made known to man before they occurred. Respecting all other events, we have no such certainty; "we know not what will be on the morrow:" "we know not what a day will bring forth." In this difference both the wisdom and goodness of God appear. It is all important that we should know the moral law, according to which, our eternal state is soon to be unalterably fixed; but a full and perfect knowledge of future events could do us no good; and in most cases would add to our misery. It is enough for us to know that a life of sin, of impenitence and unbelief, will lead to eternal misery and disgrace; that a life of holiness and faith in the Son of God, will conduct to happiness and glory. Whether our life is to be long or short, spent in sickness or in health, in affluence, or in indigence, we do not know: we may cheerfully leave the dispensations of providence to Him who worketh all things after the counsel of his own wisdom. The laws of providence being unknown to us, cannot, for this reason, be the rule of our conduct. There is no reward promised to those who fulfil these designs; nor any threatenings uttered against those who, if they could, would disobey those laws, and frustrate these designs. Things inanimate, of course incapable of rewards or punishments, obey the will of God, in the great work of providence. When the agency of man is employed, no reward is bestowed for this agency. In this respect man is like the hail, the snow, and the vapour. The only difference is, that man, being a rational creature, of course a moral agent, the wisdom of God has to secure his instrumentality, without impairing or suspending this reason, or this moral agency. To accomplish this with certainty, and to any considerable degree, would be difficult and even impossible to man. And yet something like it is often attempted, and in some degree effected, by judicious and affectionate parents, in the management of their children. Without positive restraint or coercion, by observing their disposition, by skilful arrangements, children are often induced to act that part which is agreeable to the will of their parents. In such instances, children are not sensible of the influence of parental authority; to themselves they appear to act, and in fact do act, according to their own choice; when it is certain that without this parental influence, they would have acted a different part. Now, that which parents can effect, in some degree in their children, we think is neither impossible nor even difficult for the wisdom of God to effect in men, with absolute certainty, and in any degree which the designs of his providence may require. He who formed the rational soul, knows how to reach and influence that soul, without destroying its rationality, and without its being sensible of that influence; and yet without this it would have thought, and designed, and acted differently. That this was the case with Cyrus, is undeniable; and I repeat, what has been effected in one individual may be, and no doubt is, effected in all others.

The great laws of the moral government are all certain, fixed, and immutable. They are, with propriety, said to be a transcript of the moral perfections of the Lawgiver. Man, whose knowledge is very limited, and who may become wiser by experience, may, and ought to change his laws when he discovers their imperfection but the wisdom and goodness of God are no greater now than they were from the beginning. The conduct of his moral subjects has not taught him to make the slightest change. It was from all eternity, immutably certain, that sin of every kind and degree would be condemned; and that holiness would be approved. The finally impenitent transgressor has no more reason to expect that he will escape the righteous judgments of God, nor the sincere penitent any more reason to fear that his hopes will be disappointed, than that the divine perfections will change. These laws are the wise and holy decrees, according to which the great Sovereign will express his approbation and condemnation, and distribute rewards and punishments to his moral subjects. If these laws are thus certain and immutable, shall we not conclude that the laws of providence are equally so? The providence of God is subservient to his moral designs; the one is the end, the other is, in part, the means. Is all that relates to the end unalterably fixed, and yet the means for the accomplishment of that end left vague, uncertain, and mutable? As the events of providence take place, or approach their birth, does he receive new ideas? does he become wiser, and therefore more competent to decide what will be expedient in future? Before he determines the events of one century, year, or day, does he wait to observe the success of his plans during the century, year, or day immediately preceding? Is he merely making experiments for his own improvement in wisdom, to ascertain the best manner of conducting his providence? In short, is he a man, or is he the allwise and Almighty God? If he is God, and not man, who manages the vast concerns of providence, then the laws of that providence, equally with those of the moral government, are eternal, fixed, and immutable. These laws are the wise and holy *decrees,* according to which all events, without one single mistake or failure, ever have been, and ever will be regulated.

LETTER XI.

MORAL GOVERNMENT.—SALVATION BY GRACE.

A few remarks will now be offered respecting the moral government of God; or rather respecting

THE DIVINE PURPOSE.

the redemption of man through a divine Saviour; the renovation of his heart; his restoration to the favour of God; and his preparation for eternal glory. May the Holy Spirit enlighten and assist both the writer and the reader!

"By grace ye are saved," may be the basis of these remarks. Grace, in this passage, means the free, unmerited favour of God. Salvation is an unmerited favour. Not one of the human race either does, or can deserve it; nor can they, by all that they can do, or suffer, have the shadow of a claim to it. If they could, it would then be merited; if merited, it would be a just debt; and if a debt, it could be no more grace; and if not of grace, then the passage just quoted, together with many others, should be stricken from the sacred pages. If it were a debt, then the sinner need no longer assume the attitude of an humble suppliant, humbly begging for salvation as a favour; he might approach his Judge with all the confidence of a claimant, and boldly demand what was his right; he need no longer apply to the mercy of God, but to his justice. If it were a debt, or deserved, then God is bound to pay it; for "the Judge of all the earth will do right;" then it would be no longer free, but the result of obligation. He who brings another under obligation, must confer some favour, or in some way or other, be profitable to him who is laid under obligation: but what favour can a sinner bestow; in what way can he be profitable to his Maker? He who induces another to act differently from what was intended, must present reasons of greater wisdom, and greater weight, than those possessed by him whose intention is changed: who then can induce the Almighty to act differently from his own free and sovereign pleasure? The truth is, which we shall soon feel and acknowledge, in the sincere penitence of our hearts, or in the anguish and despair of our eternal existence, that so far from deserving salvation, we deserve the righteous indignation of God, just in proportion to our guilt: for " the wages of sin is death." " Every sin deserves God's wrath and curse, both in this world and in that which is to come." Now, as we have all sinned, we all deserve to perish. This is the miserable and helpless state in which all mankind are by nature. Were it otherwise, we should not need a Saviour; salvation, in the evangelical sense, would be impossible. Every sin, therefore, that is forgiven, must be forgiven through grace; every sinner that is saved, must be saved by grace; not one of them does or can deserve it.

Of the same import is another declaration of the apostle Paul: "Eternal life is the gift of God." The disciples of Christ are now in possession of this gift; for "he who believeth on the Son hath everlasting life." Therefore this gift includes every thing pertaining to our salvation, the means and the agency by which we are united to Christ, and reconciled to God. The character, the dispositions and affections, and all the qualifications which fit us for the service of God here, and for the enjoyment of him hereafter—all are the gift of God. Accordingly we find from Scripture that all these things, in detail, are explicitly ascribed to God as his gift. The Saviour himself is the gift of God; and in him are included all things else necessary to salvation. The Holy Spirit, including all his influences, is given of God, to those who ask him. The Bible itself, with all its threatenings, admonitions, and warnings; with all its promises and invitations, its doctrines and precepts, its examples of obedience and rebellion, of holiness and sin; by which we are enlightened, impressed, and governed; by which we are wounded and healed, alarmed and comforted—the Bible is the gift of God to an ignorant, sinful, and perishing world. The holy Sabbath, so conducive to the existence and progress of vital godliness, is the ordinance of heaven. Public worship, family and private devotion, are institutions of infinite wisdom, for the perfecting of his saints. Prayer is not only an important duty, but a precious privilege, granted to us by the Father of mercies. Are we convinced of sin? it is by the Spirit, the Comforter, who is the gift of God; it is by the law which God has given us. Are we enabled to exercise faith in Christ? that faith is a divine gift. Do we love God? that love is shed abroad in our hearts by the Holy Spirit, who is given unto us. Do we sincerely repent? that repentance is given by our exalted Prince and Saviour. Are we pardoned and accepted of God? that righteousness, on account of which we are accepted, is a gift. Are we adopted into the family of heaven? that spirit of adoption we have received. Do we enjoy peace? that peace is the legacy of Christ. Have we good hope? it is given us through grace. Do we gain the victory? thanks be unto God, who giveth us the victory. All the means of grace, as they are generally called, together with all the effects which these means are made instrumental in producing on our hearts, and on our lives, are distinctly ascribed to God as his gift.

Gratitude is a sentiment awakened in the mind by the reception of favours which we esteem valuable, and which we do not deserve. Unless some favour is received, or expected, the human heart cannot feel grateful. Gratitude cannot be called into exercise by a mere act of volition, as we can raise our hand; it must have its appropriate cause. Accordingly, wherever you witness a heart expanding with its delightful emotions, you may be sure some valuable favour is either expected, or has been received. Now where is the Christian who does not feel thankful to God for causing him to differ from others; for those convictions of guilt and danger which led him to inquire what he must do to be saved; for that heavenly light which guided him safely through his perplexities and distresses, and taught him how to believe; for that gracious aid, by which he was enabled, guilty, helpless and polluted as he was, to cast himself on the merits of Jesus Christ; for that joy and peace which he found in believing; for that new heart which habitually inclines him to repent of sin, to abhor himself on account of it, to watch against and avoid it; for that relish for spiritual things, by which he is enabled to delight in communion with God, and in cheerful obedience to his will? Who is not thankful for those spiritual and devout affections which adorn the character, give the thoughts a heavenly direction, warm, elevate, and purify the soul; for that power by which he is kept through faith unto salvation? The man who is not thankful for these blessings proclaims his own ignorance of them, and proves himself unworthy the name of Christian. The grateful heart believes and acknowledges that all these are good and perfect gifts from the Father of lights.

All the blessings for which we are directed and permitted to pray, are bestowed according to the good pleasure of God. The very petitions which we offer up, imply that we have no right to claim them; and that when received, they must be received as free and unmerited favours. Careless sinners should pray that they might be impressed and awakened; the awakened should pray that they might be preserved from all the errors and delusions which beset their path, and enabled to believe in Christ with the heart unto righteousness; Christians should pray for a clean heart and a right spirit, for strength to persevere and increase in the ways of holiness; or rather, every person should pray without ceasing, for these and all other blessings. Now prayer has no meaning, it is mockery, unless it flows from a deep and thorough conviction that we do not possess that for which we pray; that we need it; and that we do not deserve it. I can conceive of no motive to pray for that which we already possess, or that which we do not need, or that which we deserve; for this we would not ask as a suppliant; we would demand it as our right. If we pray with the understanding, we know and feel at the moment, that we do not merit the blessings for which we pray; that God is under no obligation, of course, to bestow them. Were this conviction more deeply wrought in our hearts, our prayers would be mingled with more reverence, more humility, and more earnestness than they sometimes are. When God bestows the blessing, it is not as the payment of a debt, or a compensation for services which we have rendered, but freely and graciously.

These remarks are forcibly and affectingly exemplified in the case of the publican. His consciousness of misery, guilt, and unworthiness is clearly indicated by the distance at which he stands; by his downcast eye; and by smiting on his breast. He mentions no debt that is due him; no services, on account of which he ought to be heard, and rewarded. He confesses himself to be a sinner. Knowing that mercy was his only plea, though even this he did not deserve, with reverence, humility, and earnestness he prays—*God be merciful to me a sinner!*

Again; the whole work of regenerating and purifying the heart of man, from the first quickening touch, through every intervening stage of its progress, to the most triumphant assurance of faith, ever attained in this world, is directly ascribed to God, as his peculiar work. When " dead in trespasses and in sins; when children of wrath, it is God who quickeneth us." From the context it would appear that this *quickening* marks the first impression which changes the heart from a state of death-like insensibility, to serious reflection and feeling. Of the same import is the language of the Apostle James; " Of his own will begat he us with the word of truth." Regeneration, with all that it implies, is ascribed to God ; *we are his workmanship.* Those who believe in Christ, are *born of God.* Those who are called, are *called of God.* It is God who works in the hearts of his people the *work of faith with power;* who makes a way for their escape when tempted; who comforts, strengthens, and upholds them. If they work out their own salvation " it is God, of his good pleasure, who worketh in them, both to will and to do." Other passages to the same effect, need not be mentioned; for no Christian, I presume, is disposed to deny that all that is good, in the heart of man, is the work of the Spirit.

Let me ask you now, are these things so? Are we, indeed, saved by grace? Is our salvation, with all that it includes, a free, unmerited favour? Is our regeneration, and progress in holiness, from the first serious thought, to the last exercise of faith in this world, the peculiar work of the Spirit? I cannot deny myself the pleasure of believing that you reply in the affirmative. You not only admit that these things may be true, as you would admit respecting things with which you were not acquainted, or which you had not carefully examined; but on the testimony of your own experience, and of the word of God, examined with prayerful attention, you affirm that they are true. Then, my friend, you are a genuine Calvinist. This is the very essence of that system of doctrines called, sometimes by its advocates, and sometimes by its opponents, Calvinism. It is a matter of little importance, however, by what name any system of doctrine is called; if it is according to Scripture, it ought to be received; if it is not, it ought to be rejected. It ought to be neither defended nor opposed merely on account of the name which men have given it; but solely on account of its truth or its falsehood. Had this been kept habitually in view, half the disputes in the religious world would never have taken place; and the greater part of the other half would have been much shorter, been conducted with more meekness of wisdom, of course, been more profitable than they have been. By those who keep this rule in view, the Bible, understood in its plain and obvious meaning, is revered as the highest authority; as the only infallible guide. They imitate the noble Bereans, " searching the Scriptures daily, whether these things are so ;" if so, if found in the Scriptures, they are " received with all readiness of mind."

However, as I have mentioned the conclusion

which, in my opinion, follows unavoidably from the above premises, I will give you permission, and even request you to review this letter, with great attention, and with a reference, if you please to this very conclusion. What the result of such a review may be on your mind, I cannot tell; on my own mind it only strengthens the conviction that the preceding statements are abundantly supported by Scripture; that they are the plain doctrines of the Bible. Until I know to the contrary, I will suppose this is also your deliberate conviction. Then I repeat it, you are a Calvinist; you believe as they do.

LETTER XII.

THE FAVOURS OF GOD, BESTOWED ACCORDING TO HIS OWN DESIGN.—PURPOSE, DECREE, INTENTION, FORE-ORDINATION, &C., MEAN THE SAME.

PERHAPS you are not quite satisfied to be called a Calvinist; and do not feel altogether certain that you are justly entitled to this distinctive appellation. It is not my wish to induce you to adopt this or any similar name; my heart's desire and prayer to God, for you and for all men, is, that you may be saved; and in order to this, that you may clearly understand, and cordially embrace the truth, as it is in Jesus. Of one thing, however, I am certain; if you believe, as above supposed, you are as justly entitled to this appellation as I am, and as thousands of others are, to whom it is uniformly applied.

The salvation of sinners is the unmerited favour,

the gracious gift of God. When he bestows this gift, he either has an intention, a design to bestow it, or he has not. If he has no intention, then the bestowment of it must be what we call accidental. The efforts of man are frequently producing effects in this way; that is, accidentally. His efforts are intended to produce different effects; these which are produced are neither foreseen nor intended by him. That the salvation of a sinner should be an accidental effect of the divine operations; that while he was aiming to accomplish some other purpose, say the creation of an angel, this took place unexpectedly to him, is plainly too absurd to charge on any man. Nor can I admit that the man or angel ever existed, who could believe this respecting his Maker. If he has an intention, then the gift is bestowed according to this purpose, and in consequence of it. The very reason why the gift is conferred is the existence of this design. The intention is neither capricious nor arbitrary. It is not like what, in men, is called a mere fancy: it is deliberate; it is wise; it is holy. It is not formed and executed merely because he possesses the requisite power, and is not accountable to any creature for the exercise of that power. There is an end in view; an end infinitely worthy of his own character; an end which will justify this exercise of his power, wisdom, and goodness, in the view of all holy beings. This intention is according to the counsels of infinite wisdom; it is founded on reasons of infinite weight. It must, therefore, have been formed as soon as all the reasons, on which it is founded, were perceived and felt by the divine mind; as soon as the counsels, the deliberations of wisdom were concluded. Any other inference is altogether unreasonable. But this wisdom is not increased by experience, nor are these reasons discovered by investigation. This was perfect; these reasons existed from all eternity, with precisely the same weight which they now have. Therefore this intention existed from all eternity. The bestowment of this gift, of this divine life, is in consequence of an immutable, wise, benevolent, merciful, and eternal intention. All this, it appears to me, is plain and undeniable.

Now this intention is the decree of God. To say that God intended, and that he decreed from all eternity, to bestow a favour, is, in my view, the same thing. It is the same also with foreordination. This means the determining to bestow a gift before the time arrives, when the gift is actually bestowed. This term is used in accommodation to our weakness; for with God there is neither *fore* nor *after* ordination. What we call past, present, and future, are equally present to his infinite mind. The word election means substantially the same thing. At first view, it may appear more forcibly to suggest to our mind, in connexion with the intention, an idea either of the gift, or the person on whom it is conferred. This, however, is more owing to our inattention, than to any real difference in the meaning of these terms. If God intends to bestow a gift, that gift must as certainly be in his intention, as the bestowment of it; and the person on whom it is to be conferred, as certainly as the gift and its bestowment. To say that a thing is intended, purposed, or designed by the Almighty, is the same thing as to say, that it is decreed, or foreordained. To say that God intends to confer a favour on any particular person, is the same as to say, that this person is elected for that purpose. Of course, to say that there is neither decree nor foreordination of God, is the same as to say, that he has no intention; and that the gifts which he bestows, are given without intention. To say that there is nothing decreed or foreordained, is the same as to say, that he never intended to do any thing. To say that no person was ever elected, is the same as to say, that God never intended any person to receive his gift. The same remarks are true respecting the terms, predestination, predestinate, and predestinated; they mean the intention of God to bestow a favour, or to bring an event to pass: the favour bestowed, and the person on whom it is conferred, are predestinated for these purposes.

Any person who reads the Bible with attention, may easily perceive that the above terms mean the same thing, when applied to God and his designs. In proof of this, permit me to refer you to a few words, in the original of the New Testament:—Βουλη, according to Parkhurst, signifies design, purpose, decree, counsel. Luke vii. 30; "The Pharisees and lawyers rejected the counsel (την βουλην) of God against themselves." Acts ii. 23; "Him, being delivered by the determinate counsel (βουλη) and foreknowledge of God," &c. Βουλομαι signifies to will, to design, to will with authority, to decree, to ordain; Acts xii. 4; "intending (βουλομενος) after Easter," &c. 1 Cor. xii. 11; "the Spirit dividing to every man severally as he will" (καθως βουλεται.) Jas. i. 18; "of his own will (βουληθεις) begat he us," &c. Δογμα, derived from Δοκεω, to think, judge, to think proper, to determine—signifies a decree, ordinance, whether human or divine. It means the ordinances of the ceremonial law, as in Eph. ii. 15; Col. ii. 14; also the decree of Cæsar, Luke ii. 1, and Acts xvii.

7; also the decrees ordained by the Apostles and Elders, Acts xvi. 4. We are told, Acts xii. 4, that Herod having apprehended Peter, put him in prison, "intending (βουλομενος) after Easter to bring him forth to the people." Acts v. 28; "Behold," said the high priest to the apostles, "ye have filled Jerusalem with your doctrine, and intend (βουλεσθε) to bring this man's blood upon us." The word used in both these passages, to express the intention of man, is the same which is used respecting the Spirit, in the distribution of his gifts. 1 Cor. xii. 11; "dividing to every man severally as he will" (βουλεται) translated by McKnight and Thompson, "as he pleaseth." Or with equal propriety it might be rendered, "as he intends, purposes, or decrees;" that is, according to his own intention or decree. James i. 18; a particle of the same verb is applied to God: "Of his own will (βουληθεις) begat he us with the word of truth." McKnight renders it thus; "Having willed it, he hath begotten us," &c. that is, having intended, decreed or designed it; either of which would convey the same idea. Dr. McKnight's note on these words, is worthy of remark: "The regeneration of men is not a necessary act in God, but proceeds from his own free will. All the actions of God are perfectly free." This will, this pleasure of God, according to which his own favours are bestowed, and his own works are performed, is not expressed in the common translation, by the term intention, or design; but the same word as we have seen, in the original, respecting the will of man, translated *intending* and *intend,* is applied to the Spirit, and to God. The word *decree* is not so often used with this view as some others. The terms *counsel, purpose,* and *ordinance* are those most frequently used to express the will or purpose of Jehovah. Psalm xxxiii. 11; "The counsel of the Lord standeth for ever." The same meaning would be conveyed if the word *intention* or *design* were used for *counsel*. Isa. xlvi. 10; "My counsel shall stand, and I will do all my pleasure." My *design* or my *decree* shall stand, conveys the same idea. Acts xx. 27; "For I have not shunned to declare unto you the whole counsel of God." The Apostle means that he had faithfully explained all the great and immutable principles of the Gospel, the whole gracious plan of redemption through a divine Saviour. The same term is employed to express the result of those deliberations in which men are often engaged. Jer. li. 29; "Every purpose of the Lord shall be performed against Babylon." We have already seen with what accuracy this intention, this decree of God was accomplished in the destruction of Babylon. 1 Tim. i. 9; "Who hath saved us, and called us, according to his own purpose and grace." "In accomplishment of his own purpose and gift." The sense would be the same if the word *intention* or *design*, were used, instead of purpose.

The terms *predestinate, predestinated*, and *predestination*, are peculiarly objectionable to many pious people. I say the terms; for I hope they do not object to the meaning of these terms, when expressed in other words. Predestinate and predestinated are both used in Scripture, though predestination is not. It is, however, a word of creditable parentage, being as regularly derived from its verb, to predestinate, as intention is from the verb, to intend. If these words were correctly understood, they would cease to excite those unpleasant feelings with which, in some minds, they are uniformly associated. Permit me to introduce them to your acquaintance, not in the garb which prejudice has lent them, but in that plain and dignified dress which they wear in the sacred volume. The passages in which the word is used, are but few. Romans viii. 29, 30; "For whom he did foreknow, he also did predestinate to be conformed to the image of his Son. Moreover, whom he did predestinate, them he also called," &c. Eph. i. 5; " Having predestinated us to the adoption of children by Jesus Christ to himself, according to the good pleasure of his will." Verse 11; "In whom also we have obtained an inheritance, being predestinated according to the pleasure of him who worketh all things after the counsel of his own will." The word translated *predestinate*, is, in the original προοριζω. This verb is compounded of προ, which signifies *before;* and οριζω, which signifies to *bound, limit*, to *determine, decree, appoint.* Therefore προοριζω, signifies to determine, appoint, or decree any thing before hand; that is, before it comes to pass, or, as our translators believed, to *predestinate.* This translation is retained also by Dr. McKnight. That the word, in the passages just quoted, is used in connexion with the great subject of man's redemption, is unquestionable. Those whom God predestinated he predestinated to be conformed to the image of his Son; that is, that they should resemble the divine Saviour in their moral character; in opposition and hatred to sin; in love to God and man; in faith, zeal, and self-denial, meekness, humility, heavenly minded ness, devotion, and holiness. The grand object of this predestination is, that sinners should be regenerated, made holy, and enjoy everlasting happiness. That they might attain this conformity,

THE DIVINE PURPOSE. 107

he also called them; that is, by the preaching of the gospel, which the Holy Spirit rendered effectual in " turning them from darkness to light, that they might be sanctified through the truth." In Ephesians, the object of predestination is substantially the same; " To the adoption of sons." Those who bear the image of Christ, are children of God, and those are children of God, who bear the image of their Saviour. In the latter passages we are informed that this is in consequence of the mediation of Christ, " by Jesus Christ." We have also the origin of the whole gracious plan, stated for our contemplation. It is " according to the good pleasure of his will."

In all this I can see nothing objectionable. None will deem it objectionable that sinners should be saved; for it is a work in all respects worthy of God. Satan, indeed, with all his malice, subtlety, and power, is opposed to this work; but all the holy angels rejoice in it, and labour to promote it. If sinners are to be saved, in what manner shall this be done? Can it be objectionable that in order to their admission to heaven, they should first be made holy; that their hearts should be so completely changed as to resemble the lovely and heavenly character of Jesus, the Son of God; that they should be adopted into the family of their Father in heaven, and trained up in the exercise of every filial affection, in habits of humble submission, and cheerful obedience to the divine will? If they are to be made holy, by what means is this holiness to be produced? Can there be any objection to the Gospel, as the means of this happy change? Never were means better adapted to an end, than the Gospel is to this. By the word of truth they are begotten, born again, sanctified, saved. By the Gospel they are called, warned, impressed, invited, enlightened, comforted, animated, governed. The Gospel is the "wisdom of God," and the "power of God unto salvation to every one who believeth." Through whose friendship shall these means be provided; this "way of holiness" be marked out; this access to the Father be opened for sinners? Can there be any objection to the mediation of Christ? Before we object, let us see that our objections be well founded. Let us first be convinced that he neglects his disciples; that his ear is too heavy to hear their cries, his arm too short to deliver them, his righteousness too scanty to cover them, his blood without virtue to cleanse them. If no deficiency can be discovered, then, no objection can be made to his mediation. He was chosen of God to bring many sons unto glory. With whom is this plan to originate, that it may be unobjectionable to us? Would we be better pleased if it were a plan of our own devising? We are, indeed, generally fond of our own opinions, and the productions of our own efforts. But are we, with the angels for our assistants, competent to this task? Could we grasp the mighty subject? Could we arrange in all its parts and its provisions, a system which is to embrace the world, to purify and govern the sinful, polluted heart of man, to triumph over Satan, to save the soul, reconcile the pardon of sin with the rights of the divine government, kindle in heaven its brightest glories, diffuse through the universe the sublimest joy, and operate through an endless duration? If we could not devise such a plan, let us thankfully receive it from the wisdom of Him who alone could be the author of it. If he is its author, then the whole plan must be according to his own pleasure. It cannot possibly have any other origin. It is a scheme of his own wisdom, goodness, and mercy. It is, therefore, free, in the strictest sense. As he alone could devise this plan, so he alone can execute it. Men and angels are as absolutely unable to accomplish this merciful design as they are to devise it. If it is accomplished, it must be done by divine power. If sinners are saved, they must be saved by grace. The whole, from first to last, is according to his good pleasure, to the counsel of his will. If he saves sinners, it must be according to his own intention or according to the intention of others, or it must be without intention. The absurdity of this last supposition we have already seen. It is equally absurd to suppose that in saving sinners he works according to the plan, the intention, or pleasure of others, who of course, must be his creatures, and who can exercise no wisdom but what he was pleased to give them. There is no escaping therefore, from the conclusion that in the salvation of sinners, he works according to his own design; and that this design existed from all eternity. This is the predestination of the New Testament. Eternal life is the gift of God. He could not bestow this gift without an intention to do so. If such was his intention, he must also have intended some person or persons to receive this gift. Now, as far as I can see, it will convey precisely the same idea, to say that these persons were *destinated* to this end. The verb, to *destinate*, according to Dr. Johnson, signifies " to design for any particular end." And if the destination of these persons existed in the divine mind, before they received this gift, as it most unquestionably did; then no word in the English language can express more clearly that act of God, by which they were mark ed out, than the word, predestinate. Like the word in the original, of which this is a correct translation, it is compounded of *pre*, which, though not used separately in our language, signifies, *before*—generally adding to the word to which it is prefixed the idea of priority of time, and *destinate*, which is to design to a particular end. Predestinate, therefore, signifies to design before hand, any person or thing to a particular end. Can we suppose that the intention to bestow eternal life, was fixed in the divine mind from all eternity, but that the persons who were to receive this gift were left undetermined, till the very moment when the gift was bestowed? Could his wisdom or knowledge be greater at that moment than they were before? If not, he could be no better qualified to make the most proper determination, than he was before; of course, he could have no reasons for doing it, at this moment, which were not present to his mind before the foundation of the world. And neither men nor angels can conceive a motive for delaying this determination after all the reasons on which it is founded are fully possessed.

Such are my views of truth, clearly taught in the Bible, respecting the salvation of sinners. All who believe that God bestows his favours in consequence of an intention, previously existing in his mind; and that this intention embraces not only the gifts bestowed, but also the persons on whom they are conferred, are Predestinarians and Calvinists. Those who deny the doctrine of predestination, of course, deny, in my opinion, that God ever bestowed any favours on the human race; or affirm that, if he has conferred any favours, he has done it without an intention of doing so. To say that God has bestowed no favours, is to deny that any of the human race have been, or will be saved; for if saved, it must be by grace, which is unmerited favour. To say that this grace is given without design, is to say that when God saves sinners, he does not intend to do it; of course, it must be, what is generally called, accidental. From such a work, effected without design, could he either expect or derive glory, honour, and praise? But the Lord Jesus Christ did not come into this world, did not suffer and die, did not rise from the dead and ascend to heaven; the Holy Spirit does not enlighten, impress and change the heart; the Bible was not given and is not preserved; God does not pardon, preserve, and glorify his people— by accident. The whole is from design; and that design is eternal.

LETTER XIII.

THE NUMBER TO BE SAVED DEPENDS ENTIRELY ON THE WILL OF GOD.

Let me, for the sake of further illustration, suppose that the whole human race consisted of *one thousand* individuals. They are all sinners against God; are under sentence of condemnation, and deserve to perish. They are naturally and strongly inclined to sin; their hearts being governed by an active opposition to the moral character and government of God, which prompts them to transgress his law. According to their view, the law of God is contrary to their interest; because it forbids those pleasures which they love, and are endeavouring to enjoy. They delight in those things which this law condemns, and hate those which it enjoins. They therefore hate, not only this law itself, but also the government to which it belongs, and the perfections of God from which it flows. They desire not the knowledge of his ways; they forget and rebel against him habitually. This is their nature, their employment, and their delight. Now, to my mind, it is as clear as mathematical demonstration, that the scheme of redemption never could have originated with them; not only because they are utterly incapable of devising the plan, but also because they are utterly and decidedly opposed to it. The very thing from which the gospel proposes to save them, is the very thing which they love; of course, if they could, they would not devise any means of deliverance from it. In proportion to their love of sin, which is very sincere, they will object to such a plan being devised and brought into operation by another. It is undeniable, therefore, that if they are saved, the plan must originate with God. But he cannot be under any obligation to devise this plan; it must therefore, be free; all the motives leading to it, and all the reasons on which it is founded, must exist in his own nature. Unless it is according to his own pleasure, it cannot be at all. Whether he will save or destroy them, depends solely on his own decisions; no creature has a right to interfere. They deserve every one of them to be consigned to endless misery. Thanks be to his holy name, he has decided in favour of mercy and salvation. His wisdom has devised a plan which will bring more glory to his name than all his other works. All that pertains to this plan, its provisions, its measures, its means, as well as the plan itself, must be according to his own decision: his will, his sovereign pleasure, reigns over and throughout the whole. It is undeserved; it is unsolicited; nay, it is even opposed by those for whom it is intended. The number to be saved, whether the whole, or only a part, depends entirely on his own will: no creature has a right to interfere with this decision. Nor can I possibly suppose that this point is left undecided in the counsels of infinite wisdom. That God alone has the right, and that he is competent to decide, is evident. If, however, it should be supposed that this point is not decided; that the great Jehovah thought proper to determine every thing else belonging to this wonderful and gracious plan, except the number to be saved; then, permit me to ask, by whom is this important point to be decided? to whom shall it be referred? Shall God, by his own wisdom determine every thing else, and refer this matter to the holy angels; leave it with them to decide? There is not an angel in heaven who would not shudder at the idea; they know too much of the infinite wisdom of their Sovereign to think of undertaking a task like this; of dictating, or even offering advice to him. What he does they approve and adore. Shall it be left with sinners themselves to decide? Let the question, then, be proposed, in succession, to each individual to answer for himself: Are you willing to be saved? Are you willing to cease from sin, and to become holy? The whole thousand would be unanimous in answering, No! They would answer according to their own nature, their own inclinations, desires, and affections, which are all sinful; each one would, therefore, without hesitation, say, No! That this is not a slanderous exaggeration, but a sober and solemn truth, the unequivocal language of Scripture and all accurate observation of human life, do abundantly prove. To suppose that a different answer would be given, is to suppose that he who gives it is not a sinner; of course, that he is not one of this thousand; or, that he does not belong to the human race. Such, then, would be the result, if this decision were left to man; for if this were the answer of each individual respecting himself, it would be the answer of the whole thousand collectively. The whole plan of salvation would fail. The sufferings of the Saviour, the proclamations of mercy, the offers of pardon, would all be in vain! Not one of the whole thousand are willing to cease from sin, or cherish one devout sentiment. They unanimously prefer the practice and the pleasures of sin; of course, reject these offers. Such is the reception with which the Gospel universally meets from man, under the influence of depraved nature.

But why should we suppose that God has not determined this point, whether the whole, or only a part of the guilty, shall be saved? Is it because he is incompetent to the task? Who then are more competent than he? Certainly it is a decision of great importance in the divine government, and ought to be made in such a manner as would best promote the divine glory. To whom is this glory more important, and more precious than to God himself? Who understands more clearly than he does, the means of securing and promoting it? Wisdom is displayed in proposing the best end, and in devising means best calculated to accomplish that end. What end can surpass the glory of God? For this purpose the universe was created; for this purpose the plan of redemption was devised; for this purpose sinners are saved: they are *vessels of mercy* which he prepares to make known the *riches of his glory.* If then it is a decision so intimately connected with the divine glory, and requires the exercise of wisdom, of the greatest wisdom, where is the creature, or where are the creatures who possess greater wisdom than God; and who could decide this point in a manner better calculated than he, to promote this glory? The collected wisdom of the universe, when compared with that of Jehovah, is less than the taper compared with the sun. Whatever others may think and say, to my mind it is perfectly clear, not only that God is competent, but that he alone is competent to decide this question.

Or shall we suppose he declines this decision because he has not the right to make it? Who then possesses this right; and from whence do they derive it? Creatures derive their existence, and all that they possess from God. If they possess this right, they must have derived it from the Creator. If he conferred it on them, he must have previously possessed it himself; and as all that he does is according to the counsels of infinite wisdom, he must have had reasons for this transfer which infinite wisdom approves. What are these reasons? Will creatures exercise this right, and decide this point, with greater safety to the divine government, and more to the glory of God, than he himself could do? Unless they could make a better decision than he could, there would be no reason for transferring this right to them; and without a reason, such as infinite wisdom will approve, the transfer cannot be made. A better decision they could not form unless they possessed greater wisdom than he does. This is impossible; for his wisdom is infinite. It requires, therefore, but a little sober reflection to see that this supposition leads to the grossest absurdity.

If then creatures attempt to exercise this right, they must have usurped it. They must arrogate to themselves the high prerogative of God, and thus undertake to prescribe to their Maker and their Judge, what he must do. For those who exercise a right, do not merely offer advice, but pronounce an authoritative sentence. Now we are perfectly sure that the holy angels will not usurp this high prerogative of God; they will not undertake to legislate for their Sovereign. If it be usurped and exercised, it must be done by men: by the very criminals whose case is involved in the decision. That they are capable of attempting such a daring outrage, is a melancholy fact. In a manner as unequivocal and as intelligible as words could be, by their confirmed disposition, and their uniform practice, they are daily and hourly declaring their disapprobation of the divine law. By their love of sin, they reproach this law as neither just nor good. Such is the madness and folly of sinners that they are capable of arrogating the right of deciding this momentous case. But what would be their decision? We have already seen that they would decide against that part of salvation which implies and requires deliverance from sin. That they would object to regeneration and holiness of heart and life, is just as certain as that, by nature, they love and practise sin. Their sentence would be according to their own character, and what they conceived to be their own interest. For it is impossible for men, or angels, or even for God himself, to love and choose, at the same time, two things so diametrically opposite as sin and holiness. Let us suppose then, that each individual gives his decision of this case, and it will be this: "I am not to be finally condemned. I am to walk according to my own lusts; to gratify my own desires; to live according to my own pleasure, without control, and without punishment." This would be the unanimous voice of the whole thousand; for their natures are all the same. This is the decision of a criminal respecting himself, whose crimes are deeper than crimson, and more numerous than the stars in the sky; whose guilt is established by testimony clearer than the sun. It is the decision of one whose character is folly, dictating to infinite wisdom. It is a weak, selfish, wicked, condemned rebel, spurning the clemency of his sovereign; claiming the privilege of prostrating the best of laws under his feet with impunity; pronouncing an authoritative sentence, which through an endless duration, is to have an important influence on the government of the universe. Now, I question very much, whether the ingenuity of man, or even the talent of an angel, could conceive a more palpable absurdity than this consummate folly and daring wickedness, usurping the reins of government from the hands of infinite wisdom and perfect goodness. The conclusion, in my view, is unavoidable, that God alone has the right to decide this point.

Let us, however, take another view of the subject. The government of moral agents is exclusively in the hands of God; from him they have received those laws by which they ought to be regulated; to him alone they are accountable. The infliction of punishment, and the exercise of mercy, are among the most important measures of all governments, both human and divine. Now, according to supposition, there are under this moral government, one thousand criminals, justly condemned, who deserve to perish. The question to be decided is, whether the whole number, or only a part of them shall be punished as they deserve, whether the whole or only a part shall be saved. Admit, for a moment, that there is neither folly, presumption, nor wickedness, in creatures deciding this case; suppose they determine the number to be saved; yet they could not possibly execute their own sentence. This can be done by God alone. Salvation is the gracious gift of God; and it is not even supposable that creatures can bestow the favour of God their Sovereign, on whomsoever they please. In executing this sentence he would not work after the counsel of his own will, but according to the will of another. While inflicting deserved punishment, or dispensing unmerited pardon, he would only fill the subordinate office of executor of the will and pleasure of others. He could not, then, with propriety, be called the Supreme Ruler; in as much as there are others, by whose decision, in these important measures, he is governed. This part of the government, so important, and so difficult, at least with man, to be administered with safety, would not be his, but would belong to those whose will he obeys. You will, at once, perceive that this violates all our ideas of propriety, and is directly contrary to the whole tenor of Scripture. Those who suppose that God himself does not decide this question, must suppose that he does not sustain the high and august character of Supreme Ruler of the Universe; that in some important measures, he is only the subordinate agent of others. Those who believe that he is the Supreme Ruler, believe, of course, that he decides respecting this and every other measure of his own government.

That the Lord Jehovah, and he alone, is competent to decide this question; that he alone has the right; that as Supreme Ruler he must decide it; appears to be the unavoidable conclusion, flowing from premises clearly established.

Another point of great importance in the scheme of redemption, is, when shall this decision be made? or when has it been made? The whole scheme will soon come to a close; the last pardon will soon be given; "the Son will soon deliver up the kingdom to the Father, that God may be all in all." The decision must be made before that day arrives. The number of those who shall " enter into the joy of their Lord," will then be completed, neither to be increased nor diminished for ever. If it should be supposed that God has not determined this matter before, he must determine it then. His determination, let it be formed when it may, must rest upon such reasons as infinite wisdom will approve; for this is the character of all his works. He does nothing in an arbitrary manner, but all things according to the counsels of his wisdom. These reasons are not discovered by investigation, nor his wisdom increased by experience. He is, then, as competent to make the decision now, as he will be at the last moment of time. But those reasons were as well known to him, were as clearly perceived, before the foundation of the world, as they are now. I cannot, then, conceive, nor do I suppose that any man can conceive, why the decision should be delayed after all the reasons on which it is founded are clearly perceived. And as it is certain that these reasons were thus clearly perceived from all eternity, it is equally certain, at least in my view, that from all eternity, this decision has been made.

LETTER XIV.

THE MEANS OF SALVATION, SUITED TO EACH INDIVIDUAL, EMBRACED IN THE DIVINE PURPOSE.

That God has appointed the means as well as the end, is a truth which ought not to escape our attention. If the salvation of sinners is an end, determined in the councils of heaven, the means for accomplishing this end, are also appointed by the same councils. These means are wisely adapted to the necessities and character of sinners. They are guilty and need pardon; they are depraved, and need regeneration and holiness; they are ignorant, and need instruction.

That mankind are ignorant, by nature, of the plan of salvation, through a divine Saviour, is an undeniable truth. That they are ignorant of the true character of God, is equally evident. Some idea of a Supreme Being may, indeed, be found in most nations: but this knowledge is so blended with error and absurdity as to be utterly insufficient to answer the purpose of a safe guide. That this is a dangerous ignorance, destructive to the soul, is confirmed by observation and by Scripture. "My people perish for lack of knowledge. Having the understanding darkened, being alienated from the life of God through the ignorance that is in them, because of the blindness of their hearts." In order to salvation it is evident that this ignorance must be removed. And as nothing but light can remove darkness, so nothing but knowledge can dispel ignorance. Without the knowledge of the Gospel, there can be no salvation; for " this is life eternal, that they might know thee, the only true God, and Jesus Christ, whom thou hast sent." This knowledge is not, now at least, acquired by miracle, but in the same way in which the knowledge of other things is obtained; by the application of the understanding; by attention and diligence in study. In order to this, the means of information must be placed within the reach of every individual. The Bible, either directly or indirectly, is the only source from whence this information can be obtained. All who are saved, must either read and understand the Bible personally themselves, or they must receive instruction from those who are acquainted with it. The determination, therefore, to save sinners, includes the means on which that salvation depends. And as there is no regeneration without the word of God; no eternal life without the knowledge of the true God, and of Jesus Christ; and as this knowledge can only be obtained from the Bible; the divine purpose includes, of course, the presentment of the sacred pages to their attention. The design of God to call, to justify, to glorify sinners, secures the existence and concurrence of all the numerous and various circumstances and events on which their acquaintance with the Bible depends. There is almost an endless variety in the circumstances and events which bring different individuals to this acquaintance; all arranged and brought into operation at the proper time, and in their proper order by the wisdom of Him, to whom " all his works are known from the beginning." Some cannot remember the time, when the care of pious parents began to store their minds with religious instruction; others arrive at maturity, and even old age, before the knowledge of a Saviour shines into their hearts.

It is not, however, the mere possession of this knowledge that will save the soul, though it cannot be saved without it. Thousands possess it in various degrees who furnish the most afflictive proof that they are "children of wrath." No degree of knowledge without a change of heart, will prepare sinners for the joy of their Lord. This change is effected by divine power; it is the peculiar and exclusive work of the divine Spirit; yet this divine Agent generally works by the use of means, and chiefly by the instrumentality of truth. That some are savingly enlightened by reading the Bible, without the opportunity of attending public worship, I am ready to admit; still it is a fact, that "it pleases God, by the foolishness of preaching, to save those who believe." By this, sinners are generally impressed and awakened, and Christians are edified. But how often has every minister of the Gospel occasion to observe and lament, that his preaching fails to awaken the careless! His most solemn warnings; his most plain and forcible representations; his most earnest and affectionate entreaties, so far as he can observe, are in vain! Sabbath after Sabbath, and year after year, many of his hearers attend and return from the house of God, in the same state of insensibility to spiritual things. That preacher who is unwilling to acknowledge the necessity of divine agency to the success of the Gospel, might almost as well acknowledge, that it is not Christ Jesus, but himself, he is preaching; that he is not making full

THE DIVINE PURPOSE.

proof of his ministry; that he only wishes to secure the unhallowed applause, not the salvation of his hearers. The belief of this doctrine is their only refuge, their only hope of success; this, in the midst of surrounding discouragements, animates them to persevere. His influences they cannot command; but they can use those means, which, through his aid, are successful. Sometimes the hearer is more attentive and serious; good and lasting impressions are made. This is often, if not in all cases, owing to a different state of mind in the hearer. Some event has occurred which has brought the mind into a more serious mood; which has drawn off the thoughts a little more than usual from the world; and thus, without changing the heart has prepared it to receive the word. Some narrow escape from danger; some afflictive dispensation of providence; something in the conversation, or example of a Christian; or some daring wickedness in a profligate sinner, may, in the hands of the Spirit, have been the means of leading to such a train of reflection as to open the heart for the reception of the Gospel. At the same time, without supposing that the preaching which he hears is, upon the whole, better than he has formerly heard, yet there may be something in the manner of the preacher, or in the sermon itself, peculiarly adapted to his present state of mind, which renders it more interesting and more impressive. Under the impulse of these impressions, though very slight compared to what they ought to be, yet the mind is excited to further reflections, and further inquiries respecting spiritual things; and is thus prepared to observe more carefully the events of providence, and to hear with more interest and more profit, the preaching of the word. Thus that insensibility of heart, and that blindness of mind which characterize impenitent sinners, is gradually, and to himself, perhaps, imperceptibly changed. At length the truth, respecting his own guilt and danger, is admitted, which, formerly, without this preparation, this opening of the heart, would have been heard with inattention, or have been rejected through unbelief. Thus he becomes the subject of those genuine convictions of sin which extort from his heart the inquiry, what must I do to be saved? an inquiry which indicates a preparation of mind to welcome the Saviour, and his salvation. By the dispensations of providence, and chiefly by the Gospel and its holy ordinances, he is brought, " labouring and heavy laden," to the " Lamb of God, who taketh away the sin of the world," in whom he trusts with an humble confidence; and finds "joy and peace in believing." He does not now, with cold indifference, merely admit that the gospel is true; he rejoices to believe and feel that it is true; he embraces, he loves, he clings to it as his only refuge, his only ground of hope. His heart is radically changed; he is a new creature; he is a Christian.

Without affirming that the Holy Spirit observes this method, in the case of every one brought to Christ; yet I am inclined to think it more generally the method, than Christians are aware of. In giving a narrative of their religious experience, they very frequently omit those occurrences and those events which produced those slight impressions, those first thoughts and reflections, which prepared the mind to receive those deeper and more perceptible impressions, with which they usually begin their narrative. The very first reflection, with the cause which produced it, ought not to be omitted, any more than those more decisive effects which flowed from it. That circumstance, or that event which proved the cause of such reflection, however trivial and unimportant it might appear, in the view of men, was appointed, in the counsels of infinite wisdom, as an important part of the means of turning the sinner from darkness to light. Without this occurrence, the reflection to which it gave rise, would not have been excited; and without this reflection, the mind would not have been disposed to hear the Gospel with the same profit; and thus it would not have been prepared to receive those deeper impressions and those genuine convictions for sin, which may be traced back, in unbroken connexion, to the first serious thought, and the cause which produced it. If that event had not occurred precisely when it did, this reflection would not have been excited; the mind would have remained the victim of that insensibility, which would have resisted the truth. Had the Gospel not been heard while the mind was in this state; or had there been nothing in the manner of the preacher, or in his sermon, adapted to this state of mind, the effect would not have taken place. Under other circumstances, and with a different disposition, the sinner might have heard, as he had often done before, and as thousands are habitually hearing, with the most stupid indifference. But the intention of God to give eternal life, secures the means of accomplishing that intention. These means wisely adapted to each individual, in all their endless variety, in their minutest details are as much according to his holy and sovereign pleasure, as the plan of salvation itself. The Holy Spirit, with unerring and effectual control, directs that series of events, that succession of means which, through his agency, becomes instrumental in promoting the moral improvement of the mind, from the very first serious reflection, to the highest exultation of faith and hope. Uncertainty respecting one circumstance, or one single event, would mark with imperfection the plan and the work of the Spirit; all the subsequent events, which flow from this as their cause, would be equally uncertain; all the impressions, all the effects, which these events are the means of producing, would also be involved in the same uncertainty. The whole work, and of course, the salvation of the soul, might, in this way, be uncertain. But it is impossible that uncertainty can belong to the designs of God: with Him there is nothing vague, indefinite or uncertain.

This conclusion I do not see how to avoid, unless we suppose that, by the grace of God, the sinner is turned into a mere machine. This, indeed, is a charge often brought against Calvinism: but it is like all other charges brought against it— perfectly groundless. It has its origin in prejudice, or in ignorance; perhaps in both. It would not be a whit more remote from truth to say, that the food which man receives, and the air which he breathes, turn his body into a statue of marble, than to say, that the doctrines of grace, usually called Calvinistic, turn his mind into a machine, without intelligence, without thought or reflection; and which can be moved only by physical force. The doctrines of grace produce their effect by calling into action, the most vigorous action, every faculty of the soul; instead of destroying or suspending, they awaken into lively exercise, all the virtuous sensibilities of the heart. They furnish the mind with useful materials for thought and reflection, while they present to the heart, objects most worthy of its affections. Wholesome food, water, and air, do not more naturally, nor more certainly, nourish the body, than the doctrines of grace improve, expand, and elevate the mind. According to these doctrines, the sinner is not driven, blindfolded, into the kingdom of heaven, nor is he bound to it, like the sacrifice with cords to the altar; in the day of divine power he is willing; he is led, not driven, by the Holy Spirit; he is drawn by loving kindness, which employs his serious and devout consideration.

For the purpose of illustrating the preceding remarks, permit me to call your attention to the case of Lydia; Acts xvi. 14. Paul, the first Sabbath after he arrived at Philippi, went out of the city, by a river side, where prayer was wont to be made, and there spake unto the women who resorted thither. "And a certain woman, named Lydia, a seller of purple, of the city of Thyatira, which worshipped God, heard; whose heart the Lord opened, that she attended to the things which were spoken of Paul." This is a short, but satisfactory account of Lydia's first acquaintance with the Gospel, and of her cleaving to the Lord with purpose of heart. The preaching of Paul was blessed by the Holy Spirit, as the means of her salvation. Her presence, at this time, by the river side, was secured by the purpose of God, in the ordinary course of providence. Her reasons for leaving her native city, Thyatira, in Asia Minor, we do not know: probably they grew out of the trade in which she was employed. No doubt she came voluntarily, and without any expectation of what happened. The only wise God overruled the motives, by which she was induced to change her residence, to his own glory in her salvation. Her residence in Philippi, and her attendance at the place of prayer, are not only secured, but her mind also was prepared. Whose heart the Lord opened, &c. Thomson translates this, more correctly, "the Lord had opened her heart." This opening of the heart, this preparation of the mind, was a work already performed, previously to her attendance on this occasion. He who called Paul to come over into Macedonia, and who called Lydia, though in a different way, from Thyatira to Philippi, had arranged all those circumstances, and brought about all those events, which were made instrumental in giving her thoughts and reflections that particular direction which left her mind in a state most favourable to receive and welcome the messages of mercy. Under the same unerring control, Paul was led to make those remarks, to give those views of the Gospel which exactly suited her case, and which, being received by faith, sprung up, like seed in good ground, and brought forth the peaceable fruits of righteousness, the end of which is everlasting life. "The preparation of the heart in man, and the answer of the tongue, is from the Lord."

As Lydia was a free agent, she must have left her native city under the influence of motives presented to her in the ordinary way, arising out of the events of her life. Had these events been different, they would not have presented the same motives; and without motives, or reasons, she would not have changed her residence. Nor was her heart opened by any miraculous interposition, but by the blessing of God on the ordinary, perhaps, casual occurrences of life. Had these occurrences been different, they would not have answered the purpose of preparing her mind to receive the truth. Had Paul spoken on a different subject or in a different manner, not adapted to the state of her mind, the effect, without a miracle, would not have taken place. But God, who, from the beginning, had chosen her to salvation, had chosen also the means which were instrumental in bringing her, with suitable preparation of heart, to the place where she heard the words, by which she was saved. Similar attention is paid to every one who is brought to the Saviour, by Him who is wonderful in counsel.

LETTER XV.

THE PROVIDENCE OF GOD SUBSERVIENT TO THE DESIGNS OF MERCY—GREAT EVENTS MADE UP OF SMALLER—OUR DUTY AND INTEREST TO MEDITATE ON ALL HIS WORKS.

As I am not writing a system of theology, nor attempting to express my thoughts on a particular subject in systematic order, you must not be disappointed if you do not find every sentence and paragraph in what you may suppose to be its proper place. There are several considerations which I wish to suggest at present. Some of them might as well have occupied any other place: at the same time, they may be here, as well as any where else.

The subserviency of providence to the designs of mercy, has been already mentioned; and as it follows as a consequence, from the remarks of the preceding letter, I wish to offer a few further reflections on the subject. This subserviency is not only perceivable to all attentive readers of the Bible, but is frequently mentioned in plain terms. If the Lord girded Cyrus, held his right hand, subdued nations before him, it was all " for Jacob his servant's sake; and for Israel his elect." The Jews, as a correction for their idolatrous practices, are suffering in a state of bondage; the correction has, at length, produced the desired effect; and they are now to be restored to their native land, to rebuild the temple; to solemnize their annual festivals; and to reinstate the worship of the true God. In subserviency to these designs, Cyrus achieves his victories; releases the Jews from their captivity; restores them to their beloved country; even aids them in rearing the temple from its ruins; and encourages and protects them in the worship of Jehovah.

What a long train of events was rendered subservient to the removal of Joseph into Egypt! These events can be traced back to his father's partiality; to his own dream; to the envy, and unfeeling cruelty of his brethren. " They thought evil against him; but God meant it unto good—to save much people alive." Gen. 1. 20. In this the Egyptians, the most learned and refined people then on earth, had an opportunity of becoming acquainted with the character and worship of the true God. We are not informed that they improved the privilege; most probably they did not. Both nations and individuals, however, are accountable for the opportunities of improvement which are presented to them. If the means of salvation are placed fairly within their reach, they are left without excuse, though they should neglect, and even resist those means. Yet who will venture to say that none of them were enlightened by the illustrious and pious example of Joseph and his father; by the messages and miracles of Moses? The migration and bondage of the Hebrews in Egypt was rendered subservient to other great and important purposes. They were rescued from this bondage, conducted through the wilderness, and planted in the promised land, by an astonishing and constant succession of miracles. Their departure from Egypt; their passage through the Red Sea; the giving of the law, at Mount Sinai; the manna from heaven; the water from the rock; the pillar of a cloud, and of fire; are among the most astonishing and terrible displays of the divine power and glory; and continue to warn and instruct the world to this day. Wherever the Bible goes, the thunders of Sinai are heard, and its lightnings are seen. In a certain sense, the pillar of cloud by day, and of fire by night, continue to guide the people of God, through the wilderness, towards the promised land. These were, at least to the Jews, very instructive and impressive lessons; memorials of which were continued among them by divine appointment. For this purpose they are often referred to, by their religious teachers. The worship of Jehovah is often enforced, by reminding them, that He whom they are required to love and obey, is "the Lord their God, who brought them out of the land of Egypt, and from the house of bondage."

Had these miracles not been performed and recorded, the Jews, and the world, would not have received this instruction: had they not been in bondage in Egypt, the occasion of these miracles would not have existed: had the famine not prevailed, they would not have been there; for this was the cause of their going: had Joseph not been in Egypt, previous to this time, bread would not have been found, even there; for he was the means of its preservation, and thus the cause of their going would not have existed: had Joseph not been sold, and carried into Egypt, he would not have been there: had his brethren loved him as they ought; had they not envied, and hated him, they would not have sold him: had not his father loved him more than all his other children, they would not have hated him. Little did that venerable patriarch know the long train of consequences which were to flow from his fond partiality! They were perfectly known, however, to Jacob's God, who rendered this partiality, with all the consequences which flowed from it, subservient to the manifestation of his own power, his goodness and his mercy; who, in the counsels of eternal wisdom made this partiality an indispensable link in that chain of events which enlightened, and will continue to enlighten the world, till the last hour of its existence.

The first settlers of New England were induced to leave their native country by religious intolerance. At home they could not enjoy the privilege of worshipping God, according to the dictates of their own conscience. This privilege they sought, and found, in the new world. They brought with them the Gospel, with all its blessings; where it has continued to produce its heavenly effects to this hour. Those who employed this intolerance had certainly no design of spreading the Gospel to distant countries; and yet such was the effect which they were made instrumental in producing. The Most High, while he condemned their persecuting bigotry, rendered it subservient in carrying the word of life to that part of our country, where thousands have been, through its sacred influence, prepared for the mansions of glory. While man is deterred at the peril of his soul, from doing evil that good may come, it is the high prerogative of Jehovah to bring good out of evil.

The Bible Society, the greatest institution the the world ever witnessed, except those organized by special direction from heaven, may be traced back to the pious thoughts and deliberations of one single man. The Rev. Mr. Charles, while preaching in Wales, found a number of families without the Bible. He revolved in his mind, some means of supplying this want. He expressed his wishes, and his views to others; who immediately entered into his feelings, matured his suggestions, and were the honoured instruments of bringing into operation the British and Foreign Bible Society. Had those families, visited by this missionary of the cross, been supplied with Bibles, his feelings would not have been excited; for there would have been nothing to awaken them; his thoughts would not have taken this direction; for there would have been nothing to lead them. Had he not felt and thought as he did, he would not have made the suggestions which he did to his friends; without these suggestions, they would neither have matured, nor brought into operation the plan which they did; the Bible Society would not have existed; of course millions of the human family, now possessing the means of instruction, would have been sitting in darkness. But it was the purpose of eternal mercy to dispel this darkness; and with this view to bring into operation the Bible Society; not by miracle, but by human agents, influenced by their own thoughts, and their own motives;

which, had attention been paid to the subject, at the proper time, could all have been traced to some dispensation of providence as their cause. Those dispensations, or that state of things, which awakened the thoughts and reflections of Mr. Charles, have been related, are now on record, and will descend to posterity in the History of the British and Foreign Bible Society. All those events which furnished the motives by which these numerous agents were induced to act their part, were embraced in the plan of infinite wisdom, and rendered subservient to the purpose of divine benevolence in diffusing, through the world, the light of life.

Think, for a moment, of this sublime institution in embryo; when all the existence it had, except in the divine purpose, was one single thought in the mind of Mr. Charles! See this thought expanding, and producing correspondent feelings and desires; these again communicated, awakening similar feelings in other bosoms, and ripening into a plan; this plan coming into active operation, moving forward with a majesty, benevolence, and power which indicate its heavenly origin; and now, behold, the extent, the usefulness and glory of this institution, and will you not, while anticipating its complete and final success, be constrained to exclaim in the language of pious admiration, "This is the Lord's doing; and it is wondrous in our eyes!"

Mr. R. Raikes beheld a number of children, neglected by their parents, profaning the Lord's day, growing up in ignorance, acquiring habits of idleness and vice. This affecting spectacle was rendered subservient, in divine providence, to the commencement of Sunday Schools; which, through the blessing of God, have been of unspeakable use-

THE DIVINE PURPOSE.

fulness to the church of Christ. The state of the heathen, buried in ignorance, superstition, and vice, perishing for lack of knowledge, has given rise to Missionary Societies, through which the spirit of primitive piety seems, in some degree, to be reviving. Those numerous benevolent institutions which distinguish the present age, owe their origin to the miseries of man, which they are intended to relieve; and but for which, they would not have existed. These miseries are permitted to afflict one part of the human family, that the other part may have strong and rational inducements to afford relief; and thus to glorify God, by the exercise of active benevolence.

In reading the life of the Rev. John Newton, written by himself, you will find many incidents, which, at the time they happened, appeared altogether casual, and promising no very important results, yet were afterwards found to have an important influence in determining the course of his subsequent life. Had these events not happened at the very moment when they did, or had they been but a little different from what they were, they would not have produced that train of causes and effects, which flowed from them. Had the events of his life been different, his character in all human probability, would have also been different. The great Head of the Church, however, who intended him for distinguished usefulness, knew when, and in what manner, to employ the decisive control of his providence, so as to secure the occurrence of all those events furnishing all those opportunities and means of serious reflection, which, through the Holy Spirit, issued in that piety and zeal which rendered him useful to the church and to the world. So remarkable were some of these incidents, that he himself has acknowledged the hand of God in them, making them instrumental in bringing him to the knowledge of himself and of his Saviour. With this view he has pointed them out to the particular attention of his readers.

Though few men have lived a life so eventful and diversified as the former part of Mr. Newton's was, yet the providence of God extends alike to every man. Every pious man will delight to meditate on that guardian care which furnished him with the means of instruction, as well as on that divine power which rendered these instructions effectual to his salvation.

Let me recommend to you, as an employment of your thoughts both pleasing and useful, frequently and seriously to meditate on the train of events which are connected with that seriousness of mind which you now feel. According to the statement which you have given me on this subject, you need go no further back than the day on which you received the first serious impression, slight indeed in itself, but very important as it led to further inquiries on spiritual things. You have stated that you were not in the habit of attending public worship, though quite convenient to you; that on that day you had no such intention; but a neighbour, contrary to his usual custom, called, and invited you to accompany him; that there was something in the manner of this invitation which induced you to accept of it; that you returned with impressions, not very deep, but which led to further inquiries, and were increased by those inquiries. Here, with propriety, in my opinion, you date the commencement of that change of heart which you have experienced, and which, I hope, is the work of the Spirit—a radical change of character. I suppose every person will admit the correctness of your own opinion, that the public worship which you attended that day, was blessed as the means of producing that thoughtfulness with which you returned home. On how many events did your attendance on public worship that day depend? It evidently depended on the health of your neighbour. Had he been confined by sickness he would not have gone, and would not, of course, have given you the invitation which induced you to go. The sickness of his family might also have prevented him. Your own sickness, or that of some of your family, might have prevented your attending, though you had received the invitation. After you reached the place of worship, the service in which you engaged, depended on the health of the minister who conducted it. Your impressions, no doubt, depended on the sermon which you heard. Another sermon might not have had the same effect; or the same sermon from another person, might have been heard in vain. Health is evidently preserved by the providence of God; not by miracle, but by the instrumentality of second causes; by the air we breathe, the clothing we wear, the food we receive, the exercise and medicine we take, &c. These causes depend in like manner, on others which preceded them. Health, in the above instances, was preserved, not merely for its own sake, but with ulterior and more important views, that it might be subservient to the exercise of mercy. The health of your neighbour was preserved, that he might give you the invitation; your own, that you might accept of it; that of the clergyman that he might deliver those sentiments which were made effectual in awakening serious reflections in your mind. Such was the case with every individual who attended with you on that day. Such, indeed, is the case with all who, at any time, attend public worship: they are entirely dependent on the providence of God for the privilege. Our health is preserved, our life is prolonged, that we might live, " not to ourselves, but to him who died for us, and rose again." The government of providence is subservient to the work of grace; and is carried on with an evident design to promote that work.

I know that there are many pious people, and even some who hold the doctrines generally called Calvinism, who are startled at the idea of extending their inquiries into a detail of particulars. They firmly believe in the general truth, but are afraid of tracing too minutely the necessary and even scriptural inferences from that truth. Without hesitation they ascribe to the providence of God those great events which take place in the world; but they hesitate when it is proposed to investigate those minor events on which the great one depends. The life of man, they admit, is preserved by the providence of God; and yet it is with great reluctance they think of inquiring into all those second causes, all those means which Providence employs in effecting that preservation. As an excuse for themselves, and a warning, if not a reproof to others, they repeat, what, from the frequent use made of it, by respectable speakers and writers, too, they honestly believe to be Scripture, " Be not wise above what is written." Now, admitting for a moment, that this caution was found in the Scripture, I cannot perceive that it justifies this fear;

that it prohibits our inquiries into those things which are written confessedly for our instruction. I know, indeed, that there are limits; very narrow limits, too, beyond which the human mind cannot extend its inquiries with any advantage. With these good people I will unite most cordially in abhorring that rash and impious curiosity, which seeks a paltry distinction by agitating questions beyond these limits. Such discussions are not only useless, but often injurious: they may gratify the vanity of the vainglorious, but never can enlighten the mind of the sober inquirer after truth.

The life of men is preserved by the providence of God. Can it be extending our inquiries too far to ask, *how* is it preserved? Is it by miracle, or the use of means? It is certainly safe to affirm, that it is not by miracle, but by the use of means; by providing us bread to eat, water to drink, &c. May we not, with equal safety, ask, how is this bread provided? Is it possible to avoid the conclusion, that it is provided by second causes; by the labour of the husbandman, the fertility of the earth, the influence of the sun and rain. Without the influence of the sun, the rain, &c., there could be no bread; and without bread, the life of man could not long be preserved. These effects, as has already been stated, are all, in Scripture, ascribed to God; and are they not as much his work, as the preservation of life? Why then should they not be the subject of our inquiries and of our grateful acknowledgments?

These good people believe that God created the earth. But the earth is composed of hills and valleys, of rocks and mountains, and these again of atoms. Could he create the earth without creating those parts, of which it is composed? Can we go too far when the creation of these particulars is ascribed to him, as well as the earth itself? It is admitted that God " hath measured the waters," that is, the ocean, " in the hollow of his hand." In measuring the ocean, must he not measure the drops of which the ocean is composed? A house consists of a great number of parts; each of which was included in the design of the architect; and is as much the product of his ingenuity and labour, as the building itself. These parts were formed and may exist separately; but in this state they answer no valuable purpose: it is only when brought together, and arranged in proper order, that they constitute a building. When we affirm that this house was planned by the skill, and built by the labour of the architect, may we not affirm, and do we not in fact, affirm, that all the parts, even down to the minutest, were equally the product of his skill and his labour? The building could not exist without the parts; nor could the parts have existed without the design and agency of the builder. When we affirm that the life of man is preserved by the care of Providence, we, in like manner, affirm, if we understand our own language, that all the means, and all the subordinate causes, even down to the very minutest, are as certainly and as distinctly embraced in the plan, and brought into existence through the agency of God, as that preservation itself. These minute parts, these subordinate causes, cannot engage our attention at one and the same time; they may, and in my opinion ought, however, in succession. To know that our life is preserved by the constant care of heaven, is indeed calculated to excite our gratitude: but will not our grateful emotions be more sincere, more useful, because more acceptable to God, if produced by an accurate knowledge of the various means, the subordinate events combined, which are rendered instrumental in our preservation? A person viewing a building on the outside only, and at some distance, would judge that the builder was a man of skill in his profession; but his idea of that skill would be more correct and enlarged, if he should enter the building and examine each part in succession, view the neatness with which it is fitted to its place, the due proportion which it bears to each other part, and to the whole building.

Similar remarks are applicable to that work of grace, by which we become *new creatures.* This renovation is effected by the use of means. The provision, therefore, and employment of these means, by the Holy Spirit, claim our attention as constituent parts of that great work. The more extensively we are acquainted with these means, and the more diligently we use them, the more complete will the image of God be in our hearts. Great indeed should be our grateful acknowledgments to God for a new heart: but will they be less, will they not be greater, if our knowledge extends, as far as humble and judicious inquiries are calculated to extend it, to all those various means which have been made effectual in producing that state of heart; to all those different series of events, which for years, for ages past, under the control of divine wisdom and power, have been converging to this point, where a new heart, through the good Spirit of grace, is the result of their combined operation? Undoubtedly this is the way to increase our gratitude. I conclude, therefore, that such investigations, conducted with right views, and with a proper spirit, are, at once, our duty and our interest.

The philosopher who confines his attention exclusively to the planets, and other great objects of creation, may behold sublime displays of the Creator's wisdom and power. He who views, through a microscope, the wing, the joints, &c., of an insect, has an additional feast, which the former denies himself. So the Christian, who is satisfied with viewing the great events in the kingdom of providence and grace, may derive from that exhibition of the divine perfections which he perceives, the purest joy; but he who considers the smaller works of God, if the expression be allowed, has, in addition to the joys of the former, presented to his view, numberless other sources of pious delight and grateful admiration.

This was the practice of pious men whose history we have in the Bible. "I will meditate," said the Psalmist, "of all thy works: I muse on the work of thy hand." So pure was the joy derived from this source, that he wished others to drink from the same fountain. Hence his invitation: "Come and see the work of God." Hence his pious desire: "Oh, that men would praise the Lord for his wonderful works to the children of men! The works of the Lord are great; sought out of all that have pleasure therein. His work is honourable and glorious." This offers no discouragement, and still less reproof to the pious and humble student of the works of God.

LETTER XVI.

MAN IS A PREDESTINARIAN—THE COMMANDER OF AN ARMY— THE ARCHITECT—THE FARMER—ELECT, FOREORDAIN, &C.

Many of those disputes which have disgraced and perplexed the Christian world, would have been prevented, had men been required to be more definite in the meaning of their expressions. Many terms, in current use, are complex. One man includes more than another, in the meaning of such terms; of course, what one affirms, the other denies. Were both to explain their meaning by a statement of particulars, the ground of dispute might be removed. Two men will agree that God governs the world, and that we are saved by grace; and yet dispute for want of understanding the sense in which the words are used. Were they to define their meaning respectively, they would, in many cases at least, find they agree, when for want of this, they widely differ.

Last week I called to see a worthy neighbour, a pious good man. His opinions on some doctrinal subjects, and especially those called Calvinistic, are different from my own. This difference has often given rise to interesting conversations, always conducted, I hope, with the spirit of meekness and humility. It was evident his mind assumed the attitude of opposition, the moment he heard the words *election, predestination,* &c. I consider him practically right, but theoretically wrong. On his knees, and in his life, he is orthodox, whatever he may be in conversation.

He had just commenced the execution of a very

extensive plan for the improvement of his farm. Of this plan he gave me a long and particular account. For several years he had been collecting information to aid him in its arrangement: had made experiments himself, on a small scale: had carefully observed the success attending experiments made by others; and had read some of the best essays on agriculture. He had not merely resolved that he would improve his farm, leaving the means of improvement out of view, or to chance. His plan embraced a very minute detail of particulars: the implements to be used; the mode of tillage, varying to suit, as far as practicable, a wet or a dry season; the kind of crop in each field; the manner of treating his stock; were all, after mature deliberation, distinctly specified. He had made calculations of great length respecting the advantages of his plan; and his expectation was, that it would render his farm one-fourth more productive than formerly, with about one-fourth less labour.

After expressing my approbation of his plan, and my hopes that it would answer his expectations, My friend, said I, you may deny the doctrine of election and predestination, if you please; but you are a predestinarian in practice. According to the best of your knowledge, you have elected or chosen the kind of implements to be used; you have predetermined the kind of crop that is to grow in each part of your farm for ten years to come. You have stated your object, the increase of your wealth. To the attainment of this ultimate object, these decrees of your mind, and the means and arrangements embraced in these decrees, are all subservient. Why can you not permit the only wise God to act as you have done? For the attainment of a laudable end, according to the wisdom you possess, you have arranged the plan for the management of your farm, the little world subject to your control; why not permit him to have his plan arranged for the government of the universe? Having to retire, I left these remarks for his reflection.

The truth is that every man is a predestinarian in practice. As far as the knowledge he possesses will justify, and sometimes even further, he arranges his plan for the regulation of his future efforts. This plan, and these efforts, have a special reference to some ultimate object, for the attainment of which the plan is adopted, and the efforts employed.

The military chief generally forms the plan of his campaign, before he takes the field. The route by which the different divisions of his army are to move; the places where they are to be stationed; the point, when necessary, of concentration; the sources from whence supplies are to be obtained, are all predetermined. He elects to the different stations, all his subordinate officers, and assigns to each one his appropriate part of the plan for execution. Each one is furnished with the weapon he is to wield, and is made acquainted with the part he is to act. From the common soldier, up through every intervening grade, to the commander-in-chief, there is complete subordination and concert, *an army with banners.* No skilful experienced general will take the field, till these arrangements are previously made: if he should, he will probably furnish an easy victory to his enemy. and certainly forfeit his claim to military prowess.

The architect forms the plan of his building before his mechanical operations are commenced. In his own mind the building first exists, complete in all its parts. When the foundation stone is laid; when the different materials are prepared, and brought together; as the edifice rises; when it is completed; the whole is in exact conformity to his design. He will select his assistants, or subordinate agents, in performing the work; but they must obey his will, execute his plan, and not their own. Were these subordinate agents, each one, to follow a plan of his own, regardless of that of the chief architect, they would mar the beauty, and probably destroy the usefulness of the building. If success is to crown their efforts, these agents must act in complete subordination and concert; one design must regulate all their efforts. Those who are utterly incompetent to form the plan of an elegant building, may yet very well execute certain parts of that plan, when formed by another. It is possible that no person but the architect himself may have any knowledge of this plan; it may be communicated, even to the workmen, no further than is necessary for their daily operation. They may perform work, the use and design of which they do not fully comprehend. Nor is it necessary that they should, as their part is only a subordinate one; if this is well performed, it is sufficient. There are many who, for the want of some knowledge of architecture, could not comprehend the plan, if an attempt were made to state and explain it to them; and who are yet very sensible of the effect which the execution of it—which a view of the building has on their mind. When the whole work is completed, then every person may know what this plan was. The building itself

THE DIVINE PURPOSE. 147

is neither more nor less, than the accomplishment of the design, previously formed, and previously existing in the mind of the architect.

The farmer, too, practises predestination. He decrees, in his own mind, that one field shall bear one kind of crop, and another field another kind; and that he will bestow upon each the proper cultivation. The labour of every day, and week, and month, is only the execution of that design which he had previously and deliberately formed. When the labour of one day, or of one week is finished, it is not uncertain, is not left to chance, or casualty, what shall be the labour of the next. His plan extends through the whole year, and fixes the operations of each month and week. One week is predestinated to the purpose of planting or sowing, another to the purpose of reaping and gathering in the crop. The labour of one week must necessarily precede that of the following week. To neglect this order, this subordination, would be fatal to his hopes. In vain would he sow, without first preparing the soil; in vain would he expect to reap, without having sowed. His labour must not only be performed in succession, but each part of it at the proper time. If his seed is sown in harvest, it can only disappoint his expectations. No skilful and experienced farmer will neglect this order and this succession. He determines to employ such a number of labourers as are sufficient for the performance of the work. To these he makes known his plan so far as is necessary for their daily operations; further than will answer this purpose, they may know nothing of his intention. He may direct a certain field to be ploughed in a particular manner, without informing the ploughman for what purpose that manner of ploughing is required. His labourers have nothing to do with this plan, but only to execute such parts of it as may be assigned to them. At the very time they are performing their work, they may not understand the purpose which that work is intended to answer. It may have an important connexion with purposes which have not been communicated to them. They may conjecture what are the designs of their employer; but in these conjectures they may be widely mistaken. They may even censure his plan, as defective and badly arranged; but how absurd would be that censure! Let them wait till the whole plan is executed; then what formerly appeared to be defects, may become, in their view, real excellencies; what appeared badly calculated to promote his interest, or even to operate against it, may be the very measures which promoted and secured that interest. Because they are but partially acquainted with his design, they may even deny that he has any plan, extending through the year; let them wait till the end of the year, and they will see and confess that their denial proved nothing but their own ignorance.

It cannot, indeed, be affirmed of any of these designs that they are immutable, or that they will certainly be accomplished. The knowledge of men is very imperfect and very limited. In the prosecution of their designs, events which they could neither foresee nor prevent, may occur, which will render part of the means embraced in their plan, not only useless, but injurious to the attainment of their ultimate object. During their progressive operations, they may discover that, although the means employed will answer a good purpose, yet other means will answer still better. In all such cases it is their wisdom to change their plan according to this additional knowledge. Such difficulties may occur as will render certain parts of their plan altogether impracticable, which will, of course, be relinquished. But had this knowledge been possessed; had these difficulties been foreseen; had those means, better adapted to the end, been known; the plan itself, in its original formation, would have varied, just as it afterwards does when this additional knowledge is acquired. The knowledge of men, though generally progressive, is never perfect. In forming their designs they cannot employ that wisdom which can only be acquired by future experience and observation. Hence their plans often change, and some of them are never accomplished. Were their knowledge greater, their plans would be less mutable; were their power greater, they would more frequently be realized.

In the same manner, if I am not entirely mistaken, that is, according to a plan, deliberately, and previously formed, men employ their influence in attempting to change the moral character of others. The truth that they do, and that they ought, in this manner, to exert themselves, is the basis of some very important religious duties. "Train up a child in the way in which he should go:" "Parents, bring up your children in the nurture and admonition of the Lord;" are some of them. Parents generally wish their child to possess that character which they themselves most approve; because, in their opinion, this will most probably secure respectability and usefulness in life. After this model they will endeavour to form the character of their child. This opinion and this wish will decide on the plan to be adopted, and the means to be used for accomplishing this purpose. If they most approve the character of boldness and intrepidity, the actions of the brave and courageous will often be recited in language calculated to excite, in the youthful bosom, the love and admiration of these qualities; while the conduct of the cowardly and timid will be represented in colours the most repulsive and forbidding. If they wish their child to be industrious and economical, examples of these useful habits will be mentioned with the highest commendation; while the name of the idle and profligate will be associated with disapprobation and reproach. Such will be the case with parents who live under no sense of religious obligation. They will predestinate one child to be a professional character, another to be a merchant, another to be a mechanic, another a farmer, &c. But if parents themselves are truly pious, it will be the supreme wish of their hearts that their child may possess the character of genuine piety. Their plan of education will be dictated by this desire. The child will be taught to lisp the name of Jesus with reverence and delight. Examples of piety will be pointed out in the Bible as worthy of imitation. Religious friends will be received with the most cordial welcome, and spoken of with affection in presence of the child. Vice will be pointed out as dangerous and hateful. The character and example of the ungodly and wicked will sometimes be mentioned, not for the sake of invidious comparison, but of caution and warning. All their efforts will be made in consequence of their pious design to form the character of their child according to the principles of the Gospel, that it may be an active and useful member of the church, and an heir of salvation.

Ministers of the Gospel act on the same principle. All their efforts to reform and edify their hearers are according to the predetermination of their own mind. They select a subject which will furnish matter adapted to what they believe to be the general character and state of their hearers. In many instances, not only their ideas, but the words by which these ideas are to be conveyed, are carefully selected, before they enter the desk. Others who pursue a different method, arrange the train of ideas, and depend on their resources, at the moment, for appropriate language.

Such, as it appears to me, is the very nature of man, that he cannot act, at least, to any valuable purpose, without acting according to a design, previously formed. To act in this manner is one characteristic of intelligence, of rationality; and is characteristic of man, as a rational creature. The man who acts without design, who exerts himself without an object to accomplish by those exertions, is, at once, suspected of insanity. A series of exertions, subordinate to, and connected with each other, as necessarily suggests the idea of a design; and, of course, of an intelligent mind which forms that design, as an action does of an agent, who performs that action. Such exertions not only suggest the idea of a design, but of a design formed, and existing in the mind, previously to the commencement of these exertions. Whether the time which intervenes between the formation of this design, and the commencement of these exertions be long or short, cannot in the smallest degree, alter the principle. If the design existed but one hour, or even one moment before the efforts are made, its priority, in the order of time, is as real, and as certain, as if it had existed one year, or one hundred years. That the exertions are made in consequence of a design, and that this design was formed and existed, previously to the commencement of these exertions, are the points for which I contend; and which, I presume, no man of reflection will venture to deny. Of course, I can see no possible way of escaping the conclusion that man, in the constitution of his nature, and in practice, is a predestinarian. In his own mind, according to the best of his knowledge, for the accomplishment of what he conceives to be an important purpose, he decrees, he elects, he foreordains, he predestinates. He determines to accomplish a specific purpose; he selects the means, in his opinion, best adapted to this end; he employs the agency of others, without making them fully acquainted with his design, in the execution of which they are employed. Without suspending, or destroying the free agency of those whose true happiness he earnestly desires, he uses means to change and improve their character, without making them acquainted with his intention. All the actions of his life flow from these operations of his mind. Were he to act differently, he would furnish melancholy proof that he no longer retained the exercise of reason. Suppose him to act without design, and you reduce him to the grade of idiots or madmen.

If to act from design be an undeniable proof of intelligence and wisdom; if to act without design proves the want of intelligence and wisdom; then, why should we not believe that God, whose intelligence and wisdom are perfect, acts also from design? that all events, whether great or small, in our estimation; whether they relate to things temporal, or things spiritual; to the rise and fall of empires, or to the salvation of sinners; are effected according to the high and holy purpose of Jehovah, formed in the counsels of infinite wisdom, and from all eternity, existing in the divine mind? Till views of the character of God and of the meaning of the Bible, very different from those I now possess, shall reach my mind, this will be my belief.

LETTER XVII.

THE FINAL PERSEVERANCE OF CHRISTIANS.

Agreeably to your request, a few remarks will now be offered respecting the perseverance of the saints.

All true Christians are "born of God;" their moral character is radically changed; they are united to Christ by faith; for his sake, all their sins are pardoned; they are reconciled to God, and adopted into the family of heaven. That all such will continue in a state of favour with God, and finally be saved, with an everlasting salvation, is, in my view, a doctrine clearly taught in the Bible, and, therefore, "worthy of all acceptation."

Two things are essential to every Christian; a change of character and a change of state; or in other words, sanctification, and justification. These two, in the plan of redemption, are inseparably connected together: all who are sanctified, are also justified; and all who are justified, are also sanctified. Regeneration is the commencement of sanctification; and all who are "born again," are at the same time, accepted of God. Sanctification is a work: of course it admits of degrees, and of progress: justification is an act, and is perfect at once, admitting neither of degrees nor of progress. Sanctification exists in very different degrees in different individuals, and in the same individual, at different periods, and under different circumstances: justification is alike perfect in all. •Sanctification delivers from the love and practice of sin: justification, from its guilt and condemnation. The one prepares the mind for the happiness of heaven: the other gives a right to that happiness. The one is a work, effected in the heart: the other is an act of indemnity, passed in the court of heaven. That faith which " purifieth the heart, overcometh the world, and worketh by love," at the same time unites the soul to the Saviour, on whose account pardon is obtained. The best hopes of the Christian, that he is pardoned and accepted of God, rest on the evidence of his sanctification.

Now, it is the opinion of some, that Christians who have been thus regenerated, in part sanctified, united to Christ, pardoned and accepted of God, may, and frequently do, fall from grace, as it is termed; that is, that they may lose every feature of the Christian character, be completely divested of every devout sentiment and pious desire; that their hearts may again cherish a supreme love and habitual desire of sin, and be filled with enmity against God; that they may be severed from Christ, cease to enjoy the favour of God, and pass, a second time, into a state of condemnation. I will not affirm that there are no passages of Scripture which seem to support this opinion; but I think the passages which support the doctrine of the final perseverance of Christians in holiness, in union with Christ, and in favour with God, are more numerous, more explicit, and more consistent

THE DIVINE PURPOSE. 155

with all that we know of the character of God, and of the dispensation of his grace.

That some, that many thousands of Christians do persevere in holiness, to the last moment of life, none will deny. Their perseverance must depend entirely on themselves, or partly on themselves, and partly on divine aid, or entirely on the help and purpose of God. Does it depend entirely on themselves? This, I am inclined to believe, no person will affirm. Their progress in holiness is as much the work of the divine Spirit, as regeneration itself. If they work out their own salvation, it is God who worketh in them; if they live in a spiritual sense, it is " Christ who liveth in them;" " without me ye can do nothing." Does their perseverance depend partly on themselves, and partly on divine aid? This, at first sight, may appear plausible. But what part of this great and important work is it that depends on themselves? Is it their faith? This is the gift, and the work of God. Their repentance? This is the gift of their exalted Prince and Saviour. Their hope? This is given them through grace. Their love? This is "shed abroad in their hearts by the Holy Ghost." Their peace? This is bequeathed to them by their divine Friend. Their knowledge? The knowledge of God is given them. Is it their hatred and opposition to sin? This is the necessary result of those pious affections, cherished in the heart. All these things are of God; as Christians, they are his workmanship.

That there is a concurrence of their minds with the Holy Spirit, in this work, is readily admitted. Feeling the exercise of faith, they earnestly pray for its increase. Tasting the bitterness and perceiving the hatefulness of sin, they cry for help to resist its temptations and to escape its pollution. Their minds being, in some degree, savingly enlightened, they desire to grow in the knowledge of their Saviour, to abound in knowledge and wisdom and spiritual understanding. Every faculty of the mind is employed; every affection of the heart is excited. Yet this concurrence is not such as to justify us in saying that their perseverance depends, in any degree, on themselves. To the acquisition of this knowledge, to the exercise of these devout affections, to this activity and usefulness, to this perseverance in holiness, they are "constrained by the love of Christ," they are drawn by loving kindness, they are led by the Spirit. Their own agency is employed in preserving the life of the body; and yet that preservation is explicitly ascribed to God; so, the agency of Christians is employed in preserving the divine life; and yet this preservation is the peculiar work of the Spirit of God. The conclusion, therefore, is, that the perseverance of Christians, in a life of faith and holiness, depends entirely on God.

This conclusion is amply supported by scriptural authority. The prayer of our Saviour furnishes this authority. For his disciples he prays to God, "Not that thou shouldst take them out of the world, but that thou shouldst keep them from the evil. Sanctify them through the truth." The prayers of men, even of the best of men, may be so mixed with ignorance, unbelief, and imperfection, as to render them unavailing. Paul "thrice besought the Lord," without obtaining his request. Not so the prayers of Jehovah-Jesus: they are always according to the will of God; and are always heard. The Father has answered, and continues to answer this prayer. Paul affirms of the Corinthians, "ye are sanctified by the Spirit of our God." Peter declares respecting the Christians to whom he wrote, that they "were kept by the power of God, through faith, unto salvation."

If, then, the perseverance of Christians depends entirely on God; if any of them, having been regenerated, united to Christ, freely pardoned, and accepted of God, and adopted into his family, should fail to receive the end of their faith; should fall, and finally perish, it must be, either because God is unable, or unwilling to preserve them in holiness: for if he is both able and willing, then the work will certainly be accomplished; and they will receive the end of their faith, the salvation of their souls.

Now, I cannot suppose that any man with that knowledge of the divine character which the Bible furnishes, will say that God is unable to save his people from final perdition. His power can accomplish any thing which does not imply an impossibility; in the perseverance of Christians there is no impossibility; for thousands through divine grace, have persevered. The conversion of men from sin to holiness, is much more difficult, in our view, than their perseverance in that holiness; and yet this great work has been performed, by the Spirit, in the heart of every Christian. If he has performed that which is difficult, can he not perform that which is comparatively easy? The man who has raised a weight of fifty, or an hundred pounds, can he not, with the same strength, raise one of five or of ten pounds? If God has quickened the soul, when dead in sin, changed the heart, when it was in enmity against him, can he not preserve that life which he has breathed into the soul, and keep in exercise that love which he has kindled in the heart? Such is the argument of the Apostle Paul If, when we were without strength, when we were sinners, were enemies, we were made alive, pardoned, justified, reconciled to God: much more, that is, there is much greater reason to believe, that we shall be saved from wrath, through the Saviour; and in order to this, that we shall be preserved in holiness, without which none can be saved. The argument is conclusive, and unanswerable.

Besides, who are the enemies, with whom divine power has to contend? They are, indeed, numerous, powerful, malignant, and unwearied in their efforts. Satan and his legions, united with wicked men on earth, constitute a formidable host. But still they are creatures; of course, completely, and at all times, dependent on God for the power they employ against the cause of Christ. Being creatures, their power must be limited, and by consequence, less than the power of God. Will any person believe that the less shall overcome the greater? that the creature shall vanquish the Almighty? that the combined efforts of all the wicked agents in the universe, shall pluck the sheep from the grasp of Omnipotence? If Satan be a strong man armed, there is a stronger than he, to come upon him. If Satan is active and unwearied in his efforts to destroy; the Lord Jehovah is more active and unwearied to protect and to save. And, "if God be for us, who can be against us?" Therefore, we conclude respecting Christians, that "God is able to make them stand."

The willingness of God to keep his people from falling, is not less certain than his power. This is often affirmed, in the plainest terms in Scripture. Those who are called, are called according to the " purpose and grace of God. Of his own will begat he us. This is the will of God, even your sanctification." It is not a subject for investigation, but a pleasing and momentous fact, that thousands of Christians have persevered in the exercise of devout affections, and in the practice of religious duties, through all the difficulties with which they had to contend, to the moment of death. It is also a fact that this perseverance is ascribed to God, the Spirit. The man who would refuse to join in this ascription, would cast a shade of suspicion over his claims to the Christian character. If God is working in his people to will and to do, it is "according to his good pleasure;" that is, most willingly. "Thanks be to God who giveth us the victory," is the language of their hearts. This, too, is the language of heaven, where nothing but truth is admitted; "to him who washed us in his own blood," their praises are continually ascending. If, then, their sufficiency is of God; if, in a spiritual, as well as in a natural sense, "in him they live, and move, and have their being;" if their perseverance is his work, he must perform it willingly; for there is no power in existence sufficient to compel him. All his works, whether of creation, of providence, or redemption, are performed according to his own pleasure. He does not employ a subordinate agency, in executing the purpose of another; but does all things after the counsel of his own will. If he raises the soul from death to life; shields it from temptation, or makes a way for its escape; guides, supports, strengthens, and comforts it, through all the trials and afflictions of life; making all things work together for its good; and receives it finally to the joys of his kingdom; it is all according to his own purpose and grace, " which he purposed in Christ

Jesus, our Lord." If, then, God is both able and willing to preserve his people, they will be preserved.

Many passages of Scripture, if I am not entirely mistaken, clearly teach this doctrine. The Saviour, speaking of his people, says: " My sheep hear my voice, and I know them, and they follow me; and I give unto them eternal life, and they shall never perish; neither shall any pluck them out of my hand. My Father who gave them me, is greater than all; and none is able to pluck them out of my Father's hand." John x. 27, &c. The life here spoken of, is that spiritual life, obtained from Christ by faith. It is called by him who is *the truth*, eternal life; that is, it will never end; of course those who receive it, will never perish. Peter, in a passage already quoted, speaking of Christians, affirms, that they are " kept by the power of God, through faith unto salvation." 1 Pet. i. 5. Dr. McKnight, on this passage, observes, that the word here translated *kept*, " signifies *guarded in a garrison*. The term is very emphatical here. It represents believers as attacked by evil spirits and wicked men, their enemies, but defended against their attacks by the power of God, through the influence of their faith; (1 John v. 4,) just as those who are in an impregnable fortress, are secured from the attacks of their enemies, by its ramparts and walls." This passage not only affirms that they are kept, but points out the manner in which this preservation is effected; it is through faith. Now faith implies, not only the knowledge and belief of the truth, but also those pious affections and dispositions, and the practice of those religious duties which constitute true holiness. " Without holiness, no man shall see the Lord;" and without faith, no man can attain this holiness; and without the power of God, no man can exercise this faith. Believers are kept, not by miracle, nor by means which operate on them as mere machines, but by faith; by calling into vigorous exercise, every power and faculty of the soul; by exciting their desires and aversions, their joys and their sorrows, their hopes and their fears, their love and their hatred. Hear another witness to the truth of Christian perseverance. " For he hath said, I will never leave thee, nor forsake thee," Heb. xiii. 5; that is, as Dr. Scott observes, " He will not in any wise leave them, nor in any wise, on any account, in any emergency, or at any time will he forsake them. The emphasis of the original words, in which five negatives are used to increase the strength of the negation, according to the Greek idiom, can scarcely be retained in any translation." Again; Paul thanked God, upon every remembrance of the Philippians, being confident of this very thing, that " he who hath begun a good work in you, will perform it, until the day of Jesus Christ." Paraphrased thus, by Dr. McKnight: " And that he will persevere, I have no doubt; ' being persuaded of this very thing, that God, who hath begun, in you, a good work' of faith and love, ' will be completing it till the day of death;' when Christ will release you from all your trials." Now it is evident that without faith and love, none can be Christians. That he who commences, will be employed in completing this good work, till the day of death, Paul was confident; and wrote by inspiration. Doubtless, had the occasion required it, he would have used the asseveration which he did on another occasion; " I speak the truth in Christ."

We see, then, that the people of God possess

eternal life; of course, they shall never perish; for, by the power of God, they are kept, with such constancy and care, that he will never leave nor forsake them; but be engaged in completing the good work, begun in their hearts, till the day of death. These, with many other passages which might be mentioned, are sufficient to justify the persuasion, " that neither death, nor life, nor angels, nor principalities, nor powers, nor things present, nor things to come, nor height, nor depth, nor any other creature, shall be able to separate Christians from the love of God, which is in Christ Jesus, our Lord."

LETTER XVIII.

SAME SUBJECT CONTINUED.

IF Christians may, and frequently do, fall from grace, in the current sense of this phrase, they not only lose every feature of Christian character, every pious disposition, every trace of holiness, and become again totally depraved and sinful, as they were previously to their conversion; but their religious state must also be changed: from a state of pardon, justification, and peace with God, they must fall, a second time, into a state of condemnation. Their relation to God, as well as their character, must be entirely changed. Instead of sustaining to him the relation of children to a father, they must come to sustain no other relation to him than that of criminals to their judge. It has already been stated that the change of character, and change of state are inseparably connected together; and both are of grace. The life which they possess is the gift of God; and they are justified freely, through his grace. Whatever works the forfeiture of the one, does also of the other; and whatever secures the one, secures also the other. I trust it has been made to appear, that as their continuance in holiness depends entirely on God, he is both able and willing to preserve them in the exercise of holiness, so he will preserve them in a state of pardon and peace with himself; and that " there is, therefore, now no condemnation to them who are in Christ Jesus, who walk not after the flesh, but after the Spirit; because sin has not, and never shall have dominion over them." The law of the Spirit of life in Christ Jesus has made them free from the law of sin, and by consequence, also of death. I do not know that we are authorized to affirm that God might not, if it appeared good in his sight, revoke his own gifts; yet I know of no authority from Scripture for believing that he ever will. They were bestowed freely, and not by compulsion; and not inconsiderately or rashly, but deliberately, according to the counsel of his own wisdom; with a perfect knowledge of all the difficulties which might arise in the way of their continuance. Therefore we conclude that these " gifts of God," holiness and pardon, " are without repentance." Every argument which justifies our belief in their perseverance in holiness, proves also their continuance in a state of pardon; and every truth which proves their continuance in a state of pardon, confirms our conviction of their perseverance in holiness. So, on the other hand, every difficulty which forbids the supposition of their losing, or falling from the one, forbids it also of the other. Now, to me, it appears that the difficulties attending the supposition of their falling from a state of pardon and acceptance with God are very great, if not insuperable.

For the sake of illustration, let us suppose that a man lives a sinful and wicked life for thirty years, and then, through the power of the Spirit becomes a new creature, a sincere and genuine Christian. All his past offences are, of course, forgiven; for without this he could not be a Christian. Let us further suppose that he continues a Christian for one year, and then falls from grace; and that, at the end of another year, he dies, a depraved sinner, in a state of guilt and condemnation, and of course perishes for ever. Will he suffer for all his sins, or only for a part of them? for those of the first thirty years of his life, or only for those of the last year? If only for those of the last year, then his punishment would not be in proportion to his guilt; which is contrary to the principles of justice. He knew, for thirty years, his Lord's will, and prepared not himself, neither did according to his will, and yet shall be beaten with few stripes; contrary to the solemn declaration of the Judge himself. Then he will not receive according to the deeds done, that is, the sins committed, in the body, but only according to those of one year; which contradicts another decision of the Judge. For thirty years he treasured up wrath, for which no day of wrath overtakes him. For thirty years he wilfully transgressed the laws, wearied the patience and grieved the Spirit of God, and is brought into judgment and finally condemned for the guilt of only one year. Through an endless duration he will be treated neither according to the mercy nor the justice of God: mercy would save him from punishment altogether; justice would punish him for all his offences. He will neither be a "vessel of mercy," nor a "vessel of wrath." Throughout eternity the glory neither of mercy nor of justice will be displayed in his case. In this life, indeed, we behold the goodness and severity, the mercies and judgments of God, exercised towards the same individual, because this is a remedial state; but not so hereafter. In the eternal state, mercy and justice will display their glories on their own peculiar and exclusive objects; all will be either vessels of mercy, or vessels of wrath. To my mind this supposition appears utterly inadmissible. Every reason for the infliction of punishment in any degree, justifies and demands it, in exact proportion to the guilt of those on whom it is inflicted.

Shall we then suppose that he suffers for all his sins? But the guilt of the first thirty years of his life was solemnly and graciously forgiven; for, whether he had any comfortable evidence of the fact or not, without the forgiveness of all past offences, he could not be a Christian; and if not a Christian, then he could not fall from grace. He never can suffer, therefore, for that guilt which has been forgiven; for pardon is exemption from deserved punishment. Exemption and suffering; that is, to suffer and not to suffer, at the same time, and for the same guilt, is clearly impossible. Pardon is as much a solemn and official act of the Judge and Governor of the universe, as condemnation is; and all his acts are perfectly consistent. If God has justified, who is he that will condemn? For the guilt, therefore, which has been thus forgiven, the man never will come into condemnation, unless we suppose that this act of pardon shall be afterwards repealed; that what God has once solemnly and officially done, he will, in the same manner, undo; having voluntarily and deliberately declared that he will not punish, that he shall afterwards, in the same manner, declare that he will punish for the same crimes. When he made the declaration that he never would punish the man for his past transgressions, he certainly knew that, according to the case now supposed, this man would fall from grace, die in a state of sin, and finally perish; and that he would punish him for the very sins which he forgives. According to our mode of calculating time, a space of two years intervenes between the first and the last of these declarations; between the pardon and the condemnation. If a thousand years is with the Lord as one day, much more are two years as one and the same instant. As it regards the Judge himself, it is the same thing as to say that, at the same instant, he declares he will not, and declares he will punish for the same offences; at the same instant he pardons and condemns. If an earthly judge were to act thus, he ought to be instantly divested of his office, and sent to the lunatic hospital. It would grieve me to believe that a single human being, having access to the Bible, could entertain such an opinion of God his Maker.

Shall we then suppose that the pardon was conditional; and that the condition is, the man's perseverance in holiness, till the end of life? This cannot relieve us from our difficulties; it rather increases them. A conditional pardon is no pardon. Those who contend for such a pardon, can mean nothing more than the promise of a pardon for a man who will comply with the condition. But who does not see the wide difference between the promise of pardon in future, and the pardon itself which is promised? How can it produce any beneficial effects until it is passed? If it be future, how can it produce any present benefit? Your indigent neighbour comes to you almost dead with hunger, and asks you for a morsel of bread; you do not give him that which is needful for the body at this moment, but you promise that if he will preserve his life for a week, or a month, then you will give him bread. The physician finds his patient dangerously ill, and gravely promises that if he will only continue to live for a week, or a month, then an infallible remedy shall be administered. Such tender mercies are cruelties. And I feel confident that you will never mock the miseries of any human being in this manner. Pardon is an act of God. The promise to perform an act in future, necessarily implies that it is not done at present. But if it be not performed at present, the man is not, and cannot be a Christian; and if not a Christian, he can have no holiness in which to persevere. And the supposition is that he possesses holiness, is a Christian, and yet not pardoned. But the difficulties attending this hypothesis are not yet done; they rather thicken upon us as we advance. The heart of man is radically changed by the truth and Spirit of God: he exercises faith in the merits of a divine Saviour; feels a sincere love to God and man; is truly thankful for the mercies he receives; grieves for his sins with a godly sorrow; is clothed with humility; cherishes a spirit of gentleness, meekness, forbearance, and forgiveness: renders habitual and cheerful obedience to the Divine will; and perseveres in the exercise of these Christian virtues, and in the discharge of these duties till the end of life, or at least for a number of years: this is the holiness in which he is to persevere; and this perseverance is the condition on which his pardon is suspended. And yet this man is not forgiven. He is in a state of condemnation, and the " wrath of God abideth on him." He is sanctified, at least in part, but not justified: exercises all the Christian virtues: possesses the Christian character; and yet lacks something essential to a Christian; is not yet authorized to hope for heaven, because he is not yet pardoned; need not, however, fear the bottomless pit, because he is holy— But I forbear.

If the pardon of sin depends on perseverance in holiness for a time, then it cannot wholly depend on the merits of Christ nor on the free mercy and pleasure of God. But we are assured that we are forgiven for " Christ's sake:" and that for pardon we depend on the mercy of God. Besides a great many passages of Scripture declare in the most positive and explicit manner, that Christians are forgiven as soon as they believe in Christ; that is, as soon as they become Christians.

When this man shall stand before his Judge he may use this language: I have eaten and drunk in thy presence, and thou hast taught me. But the language of the Judge will be, " Depart from me thou worker of iniquity; for I never knew thee," that is, never acknowledged thee to be one of my people. Might not the man reply; Nay, but thou didst once know me. I was changed by the truth and Spirit of God; for one whole year I trusted in thy merits; felt the life-giving and purifying efficacy of thy blood; was reconciled to God through thy death; enjoyed sweet and holy communion with the Father and with thee. This would be the solemn truth. For the condemnation of this man, therefore, the Judge could not assign this reason—" I never knew thee."

It is alleged that sin is the cause of this fall from a state of holiness and favour with God, into a state of depravity and condemnation. Whether a state of sinless perfection be attainable in this life or not, I do not mean at present to inquire. I would just observe, however, that when Christians are supposed to reach that state, they cease to be objects of the divine forbearance; and it is evidently improper for them to pray for mercy. If they commit no sin, they present nothing to exercise the patience of God; they need no mercy, as they have no guilt to be forgiven. Those who contend that this state is attainable, admit that there are thousands of Christians who have not yet reached it; of course, until it is gained, they may, and actually do commit sin, and yet do not fall from grace. The advocates for this opinion allow that there may be a certain degree of sin and guilt which does not effect this terrible fall: I would ask, what is that degree, and how is it ascertained? The nature of all sin is alike, hateful to God, and polluting and dangerous to the soul. That there are degrees in guilt I have no doubt. However diversified, in our view, those opinions, passions, and practices may be which are condemned as sinful, they all have one and the same quality; and that quality is expressed by the term guilt. The fall of Christians cannot depend on the kind of sin committed, but on the degree of guilt contracted. Let us suppose that the amount of guilt which produces this fall is twenty degrees. Then it will follow that all degrees below this amount are safe, as it regards this total loss of Christian character, and forfeiture of the divine favour. Christians may commit sin till their guilt amounts to five, ten, fifteen, or even nineteen degrees, and yet they are

Christians, children of God, interested in the blood of the cross, and are objects of the peculiar favour and love of God. But if they add one degree more, then they cease to be Christians, become children of wrath, come into condemnation, and cease to be objects of the divine love and favour.

The doctrine which I defend is charged, by its opponents, with a tendency to destroy all motives to Christian watchfulness and diligence, and with furnishing inducements to a slothful and even licentious life. Now I think it undeniable that this charge, with equal force, lies against the opinion held by these opponents. According to their opinion, Christians may commit sin, may gratify the desires of the flesh, without danger of falling, until their guilt amounts to nineteen degrees, provided they do not add the twentieth.

The charge is not well founded. The former does not neglect judicious arrangements and remit his exertions, because he hopes these exertions, through the blessing of heaven, will be successful. This hope has nothing but probability for its foundation. If the probability of success prompts him to industry, then the greater this probability is, the greater will be his inducement to labour; of course, if there was a certainty that his exertions would be crowned with success, this would furnish the greatest possible inducement. And shall we say that the most powerful motive will fail, when a much weaker one will answer the purpose? that a weight of five pounds will turn the scale, when one of ten, or of twenty will not? The two cases are sufficiently similar to justify the illustration of the one by the other. The farmer has not even a probability, much less a certainty, that he will succeed without proper exertions: so he is not a Christian but a presumptuous libeller of the Gospel, who believes, or pretends to believe, that he will enjoy the happiness of heaven, without holiness, and holiness consists in the exercise of pious affections, and in the discharge of religious duties. If the farmer sows when there is only a probability that he shall reap, will not Christians " sow to the Spirit," when there is a blessed assurance that " of the Spirit they shall reap life everlasting?" The purpose of God is not to receive impenitent sinners to the joys of his kingdom, but to " save them from their sins," to " work in them the work of faith with power, to make them holy, and then admit them to his kingdom and glory."

That Christians do commit sin, is a mournful truth that cannot be denied. That their faith becomes weak, their affections languid, their exertions feeble and irregular; that they sometimes slumber, and even sleep, must be admitted. But I think it probable, that if you could ask every Christian from the beginning of the world to this day, whether his own declension in vital piety was the consequence of his understanding and believing the doctrine of final perseverance, he would answer, No; it was not. If I am not mistaken, many of those who oppose this doctrine, of course, who do not believe it, and cannot be influenced by it, experience the same chills and slumberings in their affections, and feebleness in their exertions, which are so much to be deplored in others. If then this sad decline in themselves is not, and cannot be the consequence of believing this doctrine, I hope they will not bring it as a charge against the doctrine, when believed by others. In both cases, the same effects should be ascribed to the same cause.

That some have used unguarded expressions in attempting to illustrate and defend this doctrine, I readily admit; nor will I deny that some professors of religion who live ungodly and wicked lives, may refer to their belief in this doctrine as the ground of their hope, that they will finally be saved. I cannot admit, however, that the doctrine itself is chargeable with the imprudence or absurdity of its professed advocates. The Scripture is not chargeable with the error of those who wrest it; nor the Gospel with the guilt of those who pervert its pure and wholesome instructions. I do deny that we have sufficient authority for believing that those who live ungodly and irreligious lives are Christians, whatever they may profess. They may have a name that they live, while, in fact, they are dead. This doctrine is no more accountable for their ungodliness, than the Bible which condemns that ungodliness, and which they also profess to believe. If on this account we should renounce this doctrine, we have the same reason for rejecting also the sacred volume. The real tendency of this doctrine is to be ascertained from its influence and effects on the heart and life of those who understand, believe, and love it; not from those who neither understand, believe, nor love it; and who, though its professed friends, are its secret enemies.

If it be contended that Christians may fall from grace, I would not strenuously defend the contrary position. We know that Adam fell; and we know that all sin is dangerous. Nor does it appear to me, the correct mode of speaking to say, that Christians are in no danger of falling. The sins of the children of God, as certainly meet his displeasure, as the sins of the unregenerate. Every sin is a departure from the rule of duty, according to which the favour of God may be expected. The tendency of all sin is, therefore, to separate from God. The position which I defend is, that Christians will not totally fall; and though in danger, in imminent danger, they will be shielded from that danger. Adam fell, it is true; but Adam, before his fall, though a pure and holy being, was not a Christian. No Mediator stood between him and his God; his purity was not purchased by the sufferings and the merit of a divine Saviour; no blood of infinite value was the pledge of his continuance in holiness. This, however, is the case with Christians. A divine Mediator, by his obedience and sufferings, has procured for them, complete and eternal salvation. But as there can be no salvation without holiness, therefore, holiness itself is among the invaluable blessings, procured by the blood of the cross. The covenant between them and their God, is not only ordered, but sure. The foundation of their hopes is a sure foundation. Their perseverance is secured by the death of Christ. Jehovah is their God and Father; Jesus is their Mediator, their Redeemer, their Intercessor; the Holy Spirit is their Monitor, their Comforter. The cautions, the threatenings, the warnings, the admonitions, the entreaties, the promises, the invitations, the doctrines, the precepts of the Bible, with all the dispensations of Providence, will be blessed as the means of their progress in the divine life. Not one of them shall perish; every one of them " will enter into the joy of their Lord."

LETTER XIX.

THIS DOCTRINE GIVES SUCH VIEWS OF THE CHARACTER OF GOD AS ARE CALCULATED TO EXCITE DEVOTION.—CONCLUSION.

The Bible is our only infallible guide; no system of doctrines, therefore, by what name soever it may be designated, ought to be received, that is not clearly taught in the sacred volume. By giving us correct views of the character of God, and of ourselves, by teaching us the plan of salvation through a divine Saviour, by exciting every pious affection of the heart, the Bible is intended, through the Holy Spirit, to prepare us for the worship and society of heaven, for the joys and glories of eternity. Its doctrines are according to godliness; it makes wise to salvation; it is able, or powerful to save the soul. Those doctrines which have the greatest tendency to promote holiness, are, for that reason, most worthy of our cordial acceptance. What then is the tendency of those views which have been given? In my opinion the sun is not more evidently intended, nor better calculated, to warm and enlighten the earth, the eye is not more evidently fitted for the purposes of vision, than are these doctrines to enlighten and purify the mind; to make us, and keep us sincere, humble, devout, intelligent, and useful Christians.

They represent the divine character surrounded with that glory and majesty which are calculated to excite the deepest reverence in our minds; and reverence is an indispensable feature in the character of all true worshippers of God. It is a character of fear and love. While the greatness of God bows the mind in devout awe, a view of his excellence attracts and elevates it by love. The greatness of his goodness, of his wisdom and his power, is displayed in the most impressive manner. By one single act of his infinite mind he designed the creation and government of this world, with all its numberless varieties of inhabitants, with all its countless series of events. His high and holy purpose is one! To our minds it may appear infinitely diversified, because it relates to an infinite diversity of objects and events; still, however, it is emphatically one; embracing the world with all its occurrences, through every period of its duration.

The preservation and safety of one single individual requires the concurrence of a great variety of causes, which are the effects of other causes which preceded them, still more numerous and diversified. Each of these must operate at a particular time, and in a particular order. The food that he eats is produced by the combined influence of the air, the sun, the rain, the earth, and the toil of man. The clothing which defends and comforts him is derived from different sources, and prepared by different hands. The water which he drinks is collected from innumerable veins in the earth, and presented for his use in springs and rivulets. The air which he breathes is prepared in a manner so recondite as to baffle all human discovery. Besides, he walks every day in the midst of threatening dangers, from which he must be continually shielded. All these events were designed by the wisdom, and brought to pass by the power of God, at the proper time and in the proper order.

Our impressions of greatness are often the result of comparison. Compared with the wisdom and power of God, how does the wisdom and intelligence of man disappear and shrink into nothing, and his power become perfect imbecility? The mathematical discoveries of Napier and Newton have surrounded their names with unfading renown. But suppose either of these men, distinguished for their talents, had been required to devise the means of preservation and safety to man for one single year, how utterly insufficient for the task must they have felt themselves to be! Faint, indeed, would have been their glory, compared with what it deservedly is, had it depended on their discovering the manner in which the means, provided by the wisdom and power of God, secure this preservation and safety. If the man who discovers the relation of numbers, who carries his researches a little beyond the mere surface, and discovers a few more properties of matter than were formerly known; while he confesses that there are other relations, and other properties yet undiscovered; relations and properties too, which really existed before; which he neither devised nor caused; if this man receives the applause of the civilized world; how inexpressible should be our pious admiration of the character of God, who designed and brought into existence all these relations and properties! No philosopher can devise the means of his own safety, or even comprehend how that safety is secured by the means otherwise provided. Either this invention or this discovery would raise him, in our estimation, above the grade of human beings. Yet these are the common and daily operations of Jehovah! His wisdom arranged these means, his power secures their concurrence, he perfectly understands the manner of this operation, not merely for one year, but for every successive year of life. The same wisdom, power, and goodness, have been employed in preserving all the numerous millions of mankind who have, who do now, or shall hereafter live upon the earth. The same guardian care is extended to the beasts of the field, to the fowls of the air, to the fishes of the sea, to all creeping things, to insects, to mites, though their existence should be but for a day or an hour. They are all his creatures. Their creation is embraced in his plan; so also is their preservation. Not one of them, even the smallest, is forgotten before God. The concurrence of all these causes, varied to suit their different natures, is perfectly secured by his immutable purpose. Add to this his unceasing and decisive control over all inanimate matter. The winds and the sea obey him: the torrent rushes at his command; the lightnings flash, the thunders roar at his word: the earth trembles and quakes at his touch. There is not a particle, not an atom in air, in earth, or sea, that is not as distinctly known to him, and as completely under the influence of his government, as the great globe itself. The creation, the position and movements of each atom are his work, and accomplished according to his purpose. Add to this, his influence over the minds of men, using them as instruments in effecting the designs of his providence; an influence explicitly ascribed to him in Scripture. " He fashioneth their hearts alike." " The king's heart," and by consequence, the hearts of all his subjects, " is in the hand of the Lord as the rivers of water; he turneth it whithersoever he will." Psalm xxxii. 15; Job vi. 21. " Blessed be the Lord God of our fathers who hath put such a thing as this in the king's heart, to beautify the house of the Lord which is at Jerusalem." Ezra vii. 27. This king was an idolater, not a worshipper of Jehovah; and yet what he did was put into his heart by the God of Abraham, Isaac, and Jacob. The divine influence over the mind of Cyrus has already been considered. To govern our own thoughts, affections, and desires has ever been found, if not impossible at least a very difficult task. It is only through the aid of divine grace that we can succeed in any tolerable degree. How much more difficult is it to govern the thoughts and desires of another individual. We cannot even know these thoughts and desires, except through the medium of external signs. We may indeed use means for this purpose; and our efforts may be crowned with some partial success; but to exercise a complete control over the mind of another, for one day, or even one hour, is just as impossible as to create that mind. Those things, however, which are impossible with men, are possible with God. If I have not entirely mistaken the meaning of the passages just quoted, with many others that might be mentioned, this is effected in a manner perfectly consistent with the moral agency of man, by the wisdom and power of God, just so far as the designs of his providence require; over not only one, but over each individual of the human race, not merely for a day, or an hour, but through every day and every hour of his whole life. There is not one thought conceived in the mind, that is not as distinctly known to God as the mind in which it is conceived. "O, Lord, thou knowest my thoughts afar off." "The Lord knoweth the thoughts of man." If one thought escaped his influence, so would also the consequences flowing from it. Very great events may be traced back to one single thought in the mind of some individual. One may give rise to a long train of other thoughts which, generating correspondent affections and desires, ripen into purposes, and thus lead to important results. The thoughts, desires, and affections of men are incalculably more numerous than their words and actions. The body must have rest; the tongue is often silent: but the operations and feelings of the mind are always progressing and always changing. Numerous, complicated, and mutable as they are, they are all subject to the control of divine wisdom and power. In like manner over the whole universe Jehovah reigns, with perfect ease and certainty, accomplishing his purpose without a single mistake, or a single failure.

This scheme of Providence, so vast, complicated, and incomprehensible to the view of man, is, at the same time, subservient to another plan, still more glorious, intended to display more fully the divine character, to give more correct and exalted views to man, and awaken in his heart feelings more sublime and worthy of God; that is, the plan of redemption through the cross of Jesus the Saviour. As food is subservient to the preservation of man, so the whole system of providence is subservient to the salvation of guilty sinners. In this wonderful work, sovereign mercy, forbearance, and compassion mingle their rays with those of divine wisdom, goodness, and power, and display the greatness, the majesty, and loveliness of the Deity in a light more interesting and more attractive not only to man, but to all holy intelligent beings. This subserviency and this connexion, impart to the events of time a character of greatness which they would not otherwise possess. Over this kingdom of grace, reigns a Divine Redeemer, to whom all power in heaven and earth is given; for whom, and by whom, all things, visible and invisible, were created; under whose authority all ranks of intelligent creatures are placed. This earth is but the humble theatre on which the Saviour displays and executes the designs of wisdom and mercy, in the salvation of unworthy criminals. All the great revolutions among the nations of this world are the means of promoting the prosperity of this kingdom. The commencement, the progress, and the conclusion of this dispensation of grace, will all be according to the purpose of God. The birth, the life, the sufferings, the death, the resurrection, and ascension of the Saviour were all according to the determinate counsel and foreknowledge of God. When sinners are called, regenerated, and sanctified; when they enter on the possession of their inheritance in heaven, it is according to his eternal purpose. All the means necessary to produce these gracious and glorious effects, with all the causes on which these means themselves depended, whether, in our estimation, they be great or small, are secured in their proper time, order, and degree, by the same unchangeable design of Jehovah. The day for the last act, in the administration of this kingdom, the most awful, solemn, and sublime scene the universe will ever witness, was fixed from all eternity. "He hath appointed a day in which he will judge the world." Then shall the purposes of God, requiring the existence and preservation of this earth be accomplished. Then shall all the vast and amazing schemes of Providence come to a close. Then shall the still more astonishing and glorious purposes of grace be completed. Then shall mercy have offered her last pardon, have selected and prepared her last vessel; then shall forbearance have waited her last moment; then shall compassion have shed her last tear. Then " he who is filthy, shall be filthy for ever; then he who is holy, shall be holy for ever." Then shall the kingdom be delivered up to the Father, that God may be all in all. Then shall the glory of God, the ultimate object of creation, providence, and redemption, shine forth in all its brightness. Inspired with new ardour and delight, with new sentiments of gratitude and love, of reverence and awe, then shall the heavenly hosts unite in ascribing " Blessing, and honour, and glory, and power to Him that sitteth upon the throne, and to the Lamb for ever and ever." Then shall the redeemed of the Lord add their chorus, in which even angels cannot join; " Unto Him who loved us, and washed us from our sins in his own blood, be glory and dominion, for ever and ever, Amen.'

Now, my friend, permit me to ask you seriously, what think you of these doctrines? Are they true? are they scriptural? are they worthy of God? are they consistent with all that we know of his character, and calculated to bring glory to his name? are they suited to the sinful, wretched, and helpless condition of man? are they comforting, strengthening, and cheering to the Christian? If they are, then hold fast the form of sound words and even contend, not furiously, not with the bitter zeal of party spirit, but with meekness, humility, and brotherly love, " contend earnestly for the faith, once delivered to the saints."

You ascribe the preservation of your life, and your hope of salvation to God; and for these blessings you are grateful. By this gratitude, you acknowledge that these are invaluable favours; and favours too, which you do not deserve. Will you be less thankful if you believe that they are bestowed according to an intention of your great benefactor? Will it check, will it diminish, will it not rather increase your grateful emotions to believe that this intention was formed and existed before the foundation of the world?

Let me suppose, what is not, and I hope never will be the fact, that you are in a state of indigence, suffering for the want, not only of the comforts, but even the necessaries of life; and that you shall receive something valuable from a man who is a maniac, whose actions, of course, are performed without reason and without design. In the enjoyment of what you had received you would feel glad, but not thankful, unless to Providence which controls even the actions of the maniac; but you would feel no gratitude to this man; because you would be convinced that he had no intention to relieve your distress, and felt no benevolence towards you. Even your pleasure would be that of mere animal nature, without awakening one moral sentiment of the heart. Suppose your neighbour should make you a present of such a nature, and at such time, as would justify you in saying, This is the very thing which I wanted; it is exactly suited to my necessities; my neighbour must have known my situation, and intended to relieve my sufferings. In the enjoyment of this you would feel not only the gladness of animal nature, but the most lively sentiments of gratitude, which would have an immediate object, clearly indicated by this design to relieve your wants. The knowledge of this design would have another happy effect on your mind, it would convince you that, as your benefactor was under no obligation to confer this favour, he was prompted to form and execute this **design** by pure and active benevolence. The knowledge of this benevolence would awaken your lov to the man. This gratitude and this love would increase even the gladness of animal nature, and render doubly valuable and welcome the relief you received. If your neighbour should inform you that this design had been formed a year ago; that during this time he was preparing and selecting the articles, now presented; that he only waited till the proper time should arrive, when you would be in the greatest need, when, of course, his charity would do you the most good, I venture to affirm that this information would not diminish, but very much increase your gratitude and love. If you were also informed that your neighbour was habitually engaged in relieving other sufferers, this would increase, at least, your love to the man; because it would prove that benevolence was a fixed and active principle of his heart; and that he was a worthy object of this love.

The application of this supposed case to the one under consideration, is plain and easy. God is the preserver of your life; and has given you through grace, good hope of salvation. Will not your belief, that these unmerited favours flow from design, increase your gratitude and love to your merciful Benefactor? If you could receive those favours without this belief, you could, on their account, feel neither gratitude nor love to God. Whatever gladness you might feel, it would be the gladness of mere animal nature, of the animal man, with which no devout sentiments would mingle. This belief is the main spring, is the exciting cause of your gratitude and love; because this design proves the benevolence of " the Father of lights," or as the Apostle John expresses it, that " God is love." You see the boundless exhibitions of this benevolence in the preservation of all mankind according to the wise and holy purpose of God. Look around, and you will see alas! not all, but thousands and millions of the human race, under the guidance of the Holy Spirit, rejoicing in the same hope which cheers your own heart. This will deepen the devout and pleasing conviction that benevolence and mercy are immutable and active principles in the divine character, and confirm your belief that God is, not only a proper object, but the only proper object of your supreme love.

If you believe that these favours are conferred according to design, you must believe that this design was formed, and existed, in the divine mind, before the blessings were bestowed, and if you believe that it existed before, though but for one day, or even one hour, you cannot, without the greatest absurdity, refuse to believe that it existed from all eternity. Instead of rejecting, you ought to rejoice in this belief; for it exhibits the character of God, clothed with infinite majesty, loveliness, and attraction. The preservation of your life and your hope of salvation, at this moment, depend on the means which God has employed and blessed for this purpose. These means are the effect of causes which preceded them, and these again of others; and thus, in unbroken connexion, to the beginning of time. The great Parent of the universe, with a perfect knowledge of all your necessities, looking forward with a benevolent and merciful eye, set in operation a series of events, which, under the constant guidance of his watchful and omnipotent care, has secured your present safety and happiness. The commencement of this series, with every subsequent movement and stage of its progress, is as much according to design, as are its present effects.

THE DIVINE PURPOSE. 185

Has the doctrine any thing in it forbidding and repulsive, which represents your heavenly Father, when the foundation of the earth was laid, according to the purpose of his infinite wisdom, setting in operation that chain of causes and effects, intended to issue in your temporal comfort and safety, and in your eternal salvation? If this is forbidding and repulsive, then, what is, or what can be lovely and attractive? If the design is eternal, so also are the benevolence and mercy, displayed in its execution. Can the belief that the goodness which now sustains and surrounds you with comforts, and fills you with "joy and peace in believing," is eternal, fail to have a most happy and powerful effect on your mind? Nor can you believe that the divine benevolence is an inactive, dormant principle; it is infinitely active and powerful. But how could it act in reference to you, how could it sustain and comfort you, how could it relieve your wants, until you existed and were in need of these blessing? The only way in which it could act towards you, before your life commenced, and before your wants existed, was by forming a design and making provision to watch over and preserve that life when it commenced, and to relieve these wants as they occurred. This is the very thing which has been done. This design is wise, as well as good. Divine wisdom selected the particular time and circumstances when the bestowment of these favours would produce the happiest effect not only on yourself, but on the whole universe. Had they been given either sooner or later than the time which infinite wisdom selected the good effect if any at all, must have been less than it is. And as the bestowment of these blessings is intended to impress, to warm, to expand, to elevate, and purify your heart, not only through life, but through an endless duration, it is right, it is to be expected from the character of God, that they will be conferred at the very moment when they will produce the greatest possible effect. Thus, during the current of all preceding ages, provision was making for your safety; causes and effects were maturing and converging toward the production of that hope which you now cherish; so in the events of time, provision is making for the sublime enjoyment and glories of eternity.

I cannot see how you can escape the conclusion that the benevolence, the mercy and the purpose of God, clearly displayed in your present safety and comfort, are as eternal as the divine mind in which they exist. In the possession of this belief so honourable and glorious to God, so well calculated to direct, comfort, and support you through the trials of this world, and to prepare you for the rewards of grace in the world to come, with my earnest prayers for your prosperity, both in time and eternity, for the present, I bid you adieu.

THE END.

Bibliography

1812 - *National Peace and Safety: A sermon.* Winchester, VA: J. Heiskell, 1812. 32 p.

1815 - *Memorial of Independence: A Discourse delivered in the Presbyterian church, in Shepherds-Town, (Va.) on Tuesday, the fourth of July, 1815.* Baltimore: Benjamin Edes, 1815. 23 p.

1818 - *The Duties of the Pastoral Office: A Sermon, delivered in the Second Presbyterian Church in Alexandria, at the ordination of Wells Andrews, before the Presbytery of Winchester.* Alexandria, VA: Corse & Rounsavell, 1818. 23 p.

1825 - *The Divine Purpose, displayed in the Works of Providence and Grace; in a Series of Twenty Letters, addressed to an Inquiring Friend.* Richmond, [IN]: Pollard and Goddard, 1825. 122 p.
    1828 – reprinted, Lexington, Ky.: Thomas T. Skillman, 1828. 224 p.
    1840 – reprinted, Philadelphia: Presbyterian Board of Publication, 1840. 276 p.
    1843 – reprinted, Philadelphia: Presbyterian Board of Publication, 1843. 186 p.
    2009 – reprinted, Birmingham, AL: Solid Ground Christian Books

1827 - "The Benefit of Afflictions" in *The National Preacher,* 1.9 (Feb. 1828): 129-144.

1828 - "Reconciliation by the Cross," in *The Virginia and North Caroline Presbyterian Preacher,* 1.1 (Jan. 1828).

"An Address, adapted to the Monthly Concert for Prayer," in *The Home Missionary and American Pastor's Journal,* 1,3 (1 July 1828): 41-44.

1831 - "Inaugural Address," in Cressy, Benjamin C. and John Matthews, *A Discourse on Ministerial Qualifications, delivered at Hanover Indiana, June 29, 1831.* Madison, IN: Arion & Lodge, 1831. 30 p. [marking his inauguration as professor of didactic theology in the Indiana Theological Seminary.]

1832 - "The Union of Truth and Love in the Ministry," in *The Presbyterian Preacher*, 1.3 (Aug. 1832): [33]-48. Text: 2 Cor. 6:4-7.

1833 - "Harmony of the Duty with the Promise in the Work of Regeneration" in *The Presbyterian Preacher*, 1.11 (Apr. 1833): 162-176. Text: Ezek. 18:31 & 36:26.

"Unity of Christ and the Church," in *Original Sermons by Presbyterian Ministers in The Mississippi Valley.* Cincinnati: M'Millan & Clopper, 1833, pp. 209-240. Text: Col. 1:18.

The Influence of the Bible in Improving the Understanding and Moral Character. Philadelphia: Hall, 1833. 252 pp.
    1864 - reprinted, Philadelphia: Presbyterian Board of Publication, 1864, with a memoir by James Wood.
    2009 – reprinted, Birmingham, AL: Solid Ground Christian Books

1834 - "The Deceitful and Wicked Heart," in *The Presbyterian Preacher*, 3.5 (Oct. 1834): 65-80. Text: Jer. 17:9.

1836 - "The Moral State and Character of Infants," in *The Presbyterian Preacher*, 5.6 (Nov. 1836): 85-100. Text: Luke 18:15-16.

1844 - Review of *Essays on the Church of God*, by John M. Mason, in *The Biblical Repertory and Princeton Review* 16.1 (Jan. 1844): 20-44.

Works not located:
1818 - "On Intemperance."
undated - A Biographical Sketch of the Rev. Harry Innis Todd.

www.ingramcontent.com/pod-product-compliance
Lightning Source LLC
Chambersburg PA
CBHW032115090426
42743CB00007B/358